W9-CFJ-837

Thicker Than Water
Short Stories and Poems

by
Hazel Sangster

In the dark womb where I began
My mother's life made me a man.
Through all the months of human birth
Her beauty fed my common earth,
I cannot see, nor breathe, nor stir,
But through the death of some of her.
—John Masefield

Published by

PRESS

Box 115, Superior, WI 54880 (715) 394-9513

First Edition
Published in 1996
by
Savage Press
PO Box 115
Superior WI 54880

ISBN# 1-886028-17-6
Library of Congress Catalog Card Number 96-068736

All photographs by Michael P. Savage

Printed in the United States of America

Acknowledgements

Is blood really thicker than water? In my exploration of this question, I would like to embrace my family and friends who will, no doubt, see themselves in these pages. But remember: this is fiction! My characters are always composites of many people. The situations I place them in are real or imaginary experiences taken around unexpected corners into fiction.

I would like to acknowledge Scottish traveller and story-teller Duncan Williamson, whose story *The Lighthouse Keeper,* from his collection *The Broonie, Silkies and Fairies,* I retell in *When Spring Comes;* Lewis Carroll, whose lines I use in *Lewis Carroll Defines a Father's Death;* Robert Munsch, whose story *Love You Forever* inspired *Lullabeely Legend;* and Charles Kingsley for the poem from *The Water Babies.*

Special thanks to my friends in the Copper Pig Writers' Group, the *On Spec* editorial collective, and *The Northern Reader* editors for their unflagging support, honest criticism and patience over the years. And, of course, to Mike at Savage Press.

Dedication

For my father, Alexander Brown, who
imbued me with his love of language.

Contents

Fiction

Poetry

Clear and cool, clear and cool,
By laughing shallow, and dreaming pool,
Cool and clear, cool and clear,
By shining shingle, and foaming wear;
Under the crag where the ouzel sings,
And the ivied wall where the church-bell rings,
Undefiled, for the undefiled;
Play by me, bathe in me, mother and child.
                                    —Charles Kingsley

Lullabeely Legend

There once was a little girl who loved bedtime stories and lullabies—**both** bedtime stories **and** lullabies. The bedtime story, because she loved to hear of far off places and magical people—and a gentle lullaby as her eyes grew heavy and her mind floated away.

The trouble was Mother couldn't sing—not a note. But she did like to tell stories.

The little girl lies in bed with her bear tucked into her side. Mother sits beside her, gently stroking her fine hair.

Mother and child take a trip to a wide, sandy beach where they lie on a big, fluffy towel. A hot sun beats down out of a blue, blue sky. They feel the sun hot on eyelids, neck, tummy, toes. They feel the gentle breeze blow through hair and across skin. They smell the salty air. They hear the seagulls cry. They hear the children laugh and splash in the waves that roll and crash, roll and crash, roll and crash on the smooth shore.

Outside, snowflakes dance against the bedroom window. Or the air crackles cold and clear.

One night, the little girl is a mermaid with waist-length aquamarine hair and shining silver/green tail. She swims through the white coral caverns of her father's underwater palace. The next night, she is a snowflake princess in white hooded robe. She floats in the air, dances in the wind, plays with a million snow-flake friends. She lands, one perfect, special snowflake—the only one of its kind in the whole wide world —on the black nose of a little dog.

Outside, the heat hangs heavy in the evening light and mosquitoes buzz against the screen.

The little girl grew older—and bigger. Gone was the

chubby toddler—instead braids, braces, overdue homework, telephone conversations, television shows, boyfriends, bad moods.

But she still liked a lullabeely. Sometimes, she thought it was too babyish to ask. Sometimes, the mother was too tired and cross and then, later in the evening she felt sad.

Sometimes the magic would return. Gone—tomorrow's exam, the quarrel with a friend, the ugly stories in today's newspaper. Together, mother and daughter are white unicorns, galloping across fields of red poppies. Fat fluffy clouds chasing each other and playing with the wind. Golden eagles soaring high above the glaciers.

The little girl grew up and went away to live her own life. She had her own little girl and together they made new lullabeelies. When they visited Grandma, they would lie, all three on the bed, while Grandma told an 'old' lullabeely.

The little girl and her daughter grew older, and so did the mother. Until one day she was so old, she could no longer get out of bed. She no longer *wanted* to get out of bed. The daughter came to stay. She made chicken soup and fluffed the pillows. She looked at her mother's bluely fluttering eyelids and dimming eyes and cried.

One morning, as the daughter leaned over her mother to give her a kiss, she heard the old lady whisper, "Lullabeely, lullabeely." The daughter lay down on the bed. She stroked the thin white hair away from her mother's tired eyes. She smoothed the wrinkles and worries with gentle fingers.

"It is a perfect summer day," the daughter began. The mother closed her eyes, still smiling. "The sky is blue—the kind of blue that only the sky can be. A tiny lake, still and clear, reflects the sky in its clear, cool waters. Beside the lake is a tree with shiny green leaves and pale pink blossoms. You sit, perched on the topmost branch, preparing to fly, a pure white dove..."

Motherlove

Matt broke the silence. "This is like when we used to run away from Dad."

Judy glanced over at her son sitting in the passenger seat. It was surprising that he could look so old and so young at the same time—especially in his eyes. Today his eyes, unnaturally bright and wide, made him look a lot younger than his 24 years.

"You think so?" she asked.

"Well, there's no Dad, of course. Driving up to the cabin— just you and me—" his voice trailed off.

Unhappy times, remembered Judy with a shiver, but at least those bad memories were in the past.

"Do you miss Dad?" Matt asked.

"Miss him?" Judy was surprised by the question.

"I do," Matt said before she could answer. "I know he was a shit and all that—"

Yes, he was a shit, Judy remembered.

"I hated him back then. Not anymore," Matt said quietly. "Couldn't help it, poor fuck."

Judy didn't even blink at her son's language, just nodded in agreement. Years of self-analysis and professional therapy had only clouded the issue. The only thing that she was sure about was that her husband had been a "poor fuck"—a bright, creative man in his sober moments, a crazed, yet pathetic, animal when drunk.

"Could we stop at the ICO Station in Wesley. Need to drain the lizard." Matt smiled and a dimple transformed his pale, anxious face into the winsome kid.

It was less than five minutes to Wesley but three minutes later Matt asked impatiently. "Can you drive a little faster, Ma? I thought it was closer." He fidgeted in his seat, twisting the seat belt between his fingers.

"Nearly there, Matt," his mother said quietly. The car had barely come to a halt before Matt was out the door. Five minutes later he came back, sauntering across the lot, a relaxed smile on his face, whistling. Judy sighed as she looked at him. *And their son is a "poor fuck" too*, she thought. It didn't matter anymore whether "nurture" or "nature" was to blame. The sad fact was that Matt was a drug addict, a heroin addict and there was nothing he, or she, or any of the hundreds of people who had tried to help him over the years, could do about it.

"I wanna cook dinner," Matt interrupted her thoughts. "I know exactly what we're going to have. Stop at Whitman's and I'll pick up what we need."

Judy had to smile at his enthusiasm. "Slim pickin's at Whitman's."

"Not for what I'm cookin'," laughed Matt.

A stab of regret knifed through Judy's stomach, followed immediately by the vice-like grip of anger and then bile-tasting guilt. It was all so fucking unfair and arbitrary.

Looking back, it was easy to see the warning markers. Judy looked over at her son. Matt was humming happily, looking out the window.

"Pididdle," he said, laughing, as a car with only one headlight shining in the twilight came past.

Yes, it was still easy to see that enthusiastic little kid. Despite the fact that one toy never held his attention for long and that he was too adventurous for his own good, Matt had been an easy baby, a delightful toddler—a great kid. He was always one for crazes. He would latch on to things with an all-consuming passion for a few weeks, then get bored and move on to something else. Baseball/hockey cards, hackey sack, skateboarding, rollerblading. His enthusiasm was compelling, and Judy supposed that she had indulged his lack of focus by providing him with the gear for each of his crazes.

"What are you thinking about, Mom?" asked Matt.

"I was just thinking how I always used to call you Toad," Judy answered.

"Yeah, Toad—Toady. How did I get that name—because I was a poisonous little toad?" Matt asked.

"Uh uh." Judy paused to light a cigarette. "Do you remember Toad of Toad Hall?"

"Disneyland? Toad's Amazing Ride—"

"Yes, but I used to read you the book, *Wind in the Willows*, before that. You reminded me of Toad."

"Why?

"Toad was a lovable character who lived in a big house and had these wild crazes," Judy explained. "Racing cars, boats, gypsy caravans— he was crazy about them all, but never for long. His good friends Rat and Mole tried to keep tabs on him, but he always ended up getting into trouble."

"What happened to Toad in the end?" asked Matt quietly.

"He tried to change but never quite could—I kind of like to think he did okay."

"Hope for me yet then?"

There weren't any drugs in Toad's world. Judy took a fierce draw on her cigarette as her son turned away to stare out the window. His eyes were closed and there was a faint smile on his lips. His hands, with the savagely chewed finger nails, rested quietly in his lap. The $200 she had left poking obtrusively out of her purse this morning had bought him a little peace. She remembered how horrified she had been the first time Matt filched a few bucks from her wallet for a baseball card. Over the years, she had taught herself not to count her money, so that when she had less than she expected she could blame herself for not keeping track.

"Hey, Mom—we're in Millet. Stop at Whitman's. Remember?"

Judy pulled into the small parking lot of the General Store, turned the engine off and started to get out.

"I'll get the stuff, Mom," said Matt. "A mystery dinner—alright?" He grinned.

Judy closed the car door. "OK—I'll go get gas."

Matt paused before getting out of the car, then reluctantly put his hand out. "Could I borrow some money, Mom? Pay you back when we get back to town."

"Oh right, sure," Judy pulled a couple of twenties out of her purse and gave them to Matt. "That enough?"

"Oh yeah, plenty. Want some more smokes?"

"No, I've got plenty, thanks."

Judy pulled over to the gas pumps and got out. The tank still registered at half, but she wanted to make sure it was completely filled. She went into Whitman's to pay. Matt was at the check-out looking pleased with himself. He waited with his bag of groceries while she paid.

"Oh—do you have any duct tape?" Judy asked the clerk. The young woman gestured with her head, shaking the dangling crucifix hanging from one ear. "Over there with the garden stuff." Judy found what she was looking for hanging on a display.

"What do you want duct tape for?" Matt asked.

"Last time I was up, a hose under the sink was leaking—thought this might fix it for a while," Judy explained.

Half an hour later, they were at the cabin and Matt bounded out of the car like an enthusiastic puppy. It was cold and damp inside the tiny cottage. A full moon shone across the lake ice.

"Wow," said Matt. "I love this place."

He put his groceries down. "You light the fire Mom—there's enough wood to start it. I'll go chop some more."

The wood was tinder dry and the fire sprang into life. Judy went back out to the car and brought in the water container which she installed under the sink, then made another trip for the sleeping bags and the blankets. She could hear Matt singing at the top of his lungs as he split wood.

Matt's cheeks were flushed with cold as he came in, arms laden. "That'll keep us going for a while," he said proudly. "Now, how about that leak. Let me fix that."

"It doesn't seem to be leaking anymore," said Judy. Matt peered under the sink with a flashlight. "No, it looks fine." He pulled a bottle of wine out of his grocery bag, undid the screw top and poured a glass which he brought to his mother. "Now, you just sit by the fire and enjoy this. I'm going to cook dinner."

Judy pulled the big plaid chair up to the fire and sat down with the wine in her hand. She closed her eyes. She could hear Matt rattling pots and whistling in the kitchen. As always at the cabin she had that strange feeling that life (and all its problems) was in suspension. But this time she knew they only had tonight. When the heroin bought with her $200 ran out, Matt would change into a possessed stranger who would do anything for his next fix.

"Dinner is served!" Matt announced. He had set the picnic table with a green checked table cloth and had stuck a couple of candles onto saucers. He hovered while she sat down and then served up a plate of Spaghetti-O's with a bag of sour cream and onion potato chips on the side. Judy had to smile in spite of everything.

"Bet I can guess what's for dessert." she laughed.

"Bet you can't," Matt retorted.

"Butterscotch instant pudding."

"How did'ya know that?"

"You only lived on spaghetti-O's and butterscotch instant pudding for four or five years!" Judy was about to start her spaghetti when Matt interrupted. "I want to say grace, OK? Remember how we always said grace?"

"Grace?" said Judy weakly.

"Thank you for the world so sweet. Thank you for the food we eat. Thank you for birds that sing. Thank you God for everything," Matt intoned.

The spaghetti stuck in Judy's throat and she had to turn away to wipe the tears from her eyes. The world so sweet. The world would never be sweet again. She knew as soon as Matt burst into her kitchen this morning, wolf-eyed and baying for drugs, that this was the end. It was later in the day, as Matt lay on the sofa in a drug-induced sleep, that she heard the radio report. "...break in at elderly widow's house...old woman tied up...suffocated on her own vomit... never kept any money in the house...police looking for a young blond man who was seen in the vicinity..."

After the last of the butterscotch pudding, Matt began to get restless. "Think I'll take a walk, Mom."

"That sounds nice," Judy began to get up.

"Kind of want to go alone," Matt apologized. "Mind?"

Judy sank back down and shook her head. "No—not at all—I'll do the dishes—you did the cooking!"

Matt came back in less than ten minutes, staggering a little. "I'm tired, Mom. Know what I really want?" he asked, grinning.

"Tell me," his mother said.

"I want to curl up in my sleeping bag and for you to tell me a bedtime story."

"Oh Matt," Judy protested. "I don't know if I'm up for a bedtime story."

"Please, Mom," cajoled Matt.

Judy shook her head in disbelief, laughing in spite of herself. "Oh, alright then."

Matt spread his sleeping bag on the rug in front of the fire and got into it. He pulled the edge of the bag right up so that only his eyes were showing over the top. Judy sat down beside him. "What kind of story do you want then?"

"One of your lullabeelies—I want one of your lullabeelies."

"I haven't told a lullabeely for years," said Judy quietly.

Matt's eyes, huge dark pupils, begged.

"You are on a long stretch of white beach—soft warm sand as far as you can see—lying on a soft, yellow towel. A gentle sun warms your body."

Judy gently stroked Matt's face, smoothing the silky hair back from the eyes with their fluttering lids. Her fingers smoothed the deep furrow between his eyes. "A tender wind blows through your hair, across your eyelids, your lips." She blew gently onto his face.

"You can hear the waves in the distance, rolling up the beach, one after the other, schwssshhh, schwssshhh, one after the other, rolling up the beach, hissing back."

Matt's breathing steadied as she continued. "You can hear the cries of children playing in the waves, the cries of sea gulls circling. But it's all so faint, so far away. You feel the warm sun soak into your soul— soothe, stroke, heal every corner of your body."

Matt's head relaxed to one side as she slowed her words and finally stopped speaking. He was asleep. Judy stared down at the smooth young face before getting up abruptly. She crossed to the window and opened it a crack.

Judy took the duct tape from the kitchen counter and went outside. She started the car and backed it up to the window of the one-room cabin. She turned the engine off. She got out, opened the trunk and took out the garden hose she had brought from town. Carefully she put one end of the hose into the exhaust pipe and secured it with three layers—no, four layers, of the duct tape she had bought at Whitman's. She fed the other end through the open window.

Back in the cabin she pulled the window down, wedging the hose tight and snug with two comforters and the afghan off the plaid chair. She went back outside and re-started the car, grimacing at the noise. She sat in the car long enough to make sure it was running smoothly and then went back into the house.

She closed the door tight, pushing the knitted snake draft-stopper tight along the bottom. Matt was sleeping soundly, a moonbeam illuminated his pale features. Judy stared down at him for one painful moment before lying down behind him, curling close to his body. Matt stirred in his sleep, reaching for his mother's hand to hold tightly against his chest. Judy bent her head to rest her forehead against Matt's warm back. She closed her eyes against the hot tears and pressed her nose deeper into her son's back and his familiar smell.

Self-Control

You gotta
Learn
To control yourself
Bowels
Bladder
Throwing spaghetti sauce
Throwing temper tantrums
Finger painting on the walls
Hoarding your toys
Imaginary friends
Hugging strangers
Calling out in the middle of the night with nightmare
Telling wild stories just for the heck of it
Daydreaming
Dreaming that one day you'll be
An astronaut
A lion-tamer
Sleeping 'til noon
Sleeping around
Drinking, smoking
Eating too much junk food
Eating too much fat
Eating
Watching TV
When you should be
Working out
Taking afternoon naps
Talking to yourself
Forgetting dentist appointments
Forgetting the kids' birthdays
Forgetting the kids
Dribbling on your chin
Bladder
Bowels.

My Mother...the Asshole

My mother's an asshole
(She hates that word)
Asshole—asshole—asshole

"Remember to read your answers over before finishing the exam...
Remember how much **you** hated it when bigger kids teased **you**...
You always learn more from your failures, you know...
You're never no good, **or** too good at something to learn more...
I know I bug you, but I'm not going to quit, because I love you...
I know how you feel—I **was** your age once, believe it or not..."

See what I gotta put up with?
Reminding me to wash my hands,
Eat my vegetables,
Or worse, flush
When friends are over.
Hugs in public,
Soppy little notes on my pillow if she's yelled at me,
Reading the last two chapters of my history assignment and telling
me about it as I inhale a bowl of cereal,
Forgetting I owe her five bucks, though I know she remembers
Telling Dad **she** broke the china dog on the mantel when it was
really me playing soccer in the living room.

I guess I love the old asshole...

But she's still an asshole.

My Son...the Asshole

My son can be a real asshole
That's right—ASSHOLE
That's his word for everything—including me
And I hate it.
But he's still an asshole.

"The guy's boring, history's boring, what d'ya expect me to do?
Sit still?
Everyone **else** thought it was funny...
You didn't give me a napkin and the cushion was right there...
I needed wheels for my science project and your CD's were just
the right size...
It's not my fault it snows on Mondays. I'll shovel on the weekend
Where did you put my...?"

You see what I got to put up with?
Half-drunk pop cans,
Popcorn under the cushions,
Dirty laundry,
Dirty language,
Sudden hugs,
M & M pancakes on Mother's Day,
Stuffed tiger and monkey (Tigris and Euphrates) for my birthday
"I love my old mummy bummy."

And **I** love the little asshole.

When Spring Comes

I t was the kind of room that would be described in a real estate brochure as *cozy*. Small, but not cramped, comfortably filled with old, but not shabby, furniture. At one end a bay window looked out onto the beach. Not the kind of beach from travel brochures. There was some sand at low tide, but it was mostly rock, some encrusted with barnacles and sea mosses, some worn smooth by centuries of waves. Right now the window pane was streaming with rain, the inside of the glass fogged with condensation.The only sound was the waves crashing on the rocks. A weak beam from the lighthouse flashed through the mist. The fogged hills of Mora rosethrough the clouds on the far side of the Sound, while a silent seal stared mournfully from the rocks.

Inside, a fire crackled in the fireplace. A woman sat in a tartan covered armchair in front of the blaze, reading. A man lay on a reclining chair at the window, staring out through the water streaming down the glass. An old radio played a Mozart piano concerto.

Suddenly a piercing electronic alarm signal went off, and the man and woman jumped. The woman put her book down, ran over to the man, and started fiddling with the dials on a large machine beside him.

"Don't panic, Agnes. It's just the venous pressure, again. I don't know why they make these things so sensitive—just a bloody nuisance."

"I'd better take your blood pressure, just to be on the safe side."

Agnes took a blood pressure cuff off the top of the dialysis machine and wrapped it around Ian's arm.

"It doesn't have to be that tight, woman. You're supposed

to measure my blood pressure, not cut it off—not that you wouldn't like to, of course."

Agnes clenched her teeth, then immediately forced herself to relax her jaw.

I must stop doing that. The dentist said that I was cracking my back molars by clenching and grinding my teeth. Relax. Try not to get upset. It doesn't help anybody. Ian can't help it. If you had to poke needles into yourself and lie tied to a machine three times a week just in order to live, then you'd get grouchy too and hit out at the nearest person.

A small Mickey Mouse alarm clock on top of the machine suddenly began to ring. "Time to stop the heparin."

"Stop the heparin, take two injections of interferon, half a dozen of this and bottle of anything you fancy as long as it's toxic and call me when you're dead." Ian closed his eyes.

Why do I talk like that? Look at her, cringing over the tubing. Why do I want to hurt her? She's put on more weight. Pound for pound, probably. That's where my flesh is going. She always was round. That was part of the appeal. Escape from the thin sharp perfection of my mother to those soft, dimpled, flour-covered arms. Agnes, the assistant pastry chef at the Ballachulish Hotel. Ian, the porridge pot cleaner, the toilet unblocker, in the "Ian will give you a hand" summer—but what a summer. We had our whole lives worked out then, Agnes and I. Nothing was impossible under the Northern midnight sky.

"I'm going to put the kettle on, Ian. How about I make you a bowl of chicken soup?"

"Not chicken soup again, Agnes. I'm not recovering from the flu."

"Well, what would you like? An omelette? A toasted tuna sandwich?"

"I'd like a bacon sandwich, some salt and vinegar potato chips on the side, and a mug of export.

"I'll bring you some tea and an egg."

"Don't bother—I'm not hungry for that kind of pap."

"But Ian, you have to eat."

"Why do I have to eat, Agnes?" Ian turned away and stared out the window. The rain wasn't as heavy now. The mist was clearing. It was high tide. Some yards from shore a rocky outcrop shone wet with rain and waves. A sleek, smooth seal, completely still and silent, lay on top of the rock. Its head was slightly raised and it seemed as if it was staring directly across the water, into the room, into Ian's eyes.

It's got to be the same seal. It's always on that rock at this time of tide. When I was out walking—hobbling more like— the other day—it followed me along the shore, turning to make sure I was coming, staring at me with those sad, deep eyes.

Agnes took the needle and the tubing that had carried the heparin out to the kitchen and threw it into a the "contaminated hospital waste" container. Slowly she washed her hands at the sink. Through the kitchen window she watched a lone seal swim slowly past the beach, its mournful eyes turned towards the cottage. She turned away to plug in the kettle. While waiting for it to boil, she sat at the small kitchen table, pulled a tin towards her, took out a piece of shortbread and started eating it.

Special high calorie shortbread, no salt. Just what I need. If I were ill, who would coax me to eat. I haven't been ill since I left home. That last time, just before I married Ian—I don't think I've ever been sick since then. I enjoyed that illness—hepatitis— sounded serious, even a bit dangerous. Mother came down to London to bring me home. I lay in bed, or on the garden seat, wrapped in a lambswool blanket that smelled of mothballs. I didn't read. I didn't listen to music. I slept and dozed and was an absolute bitch to my mother. She spent her nights dreaming up and her days making tasty little concoctions that I wouldn't eat.

"What are you doing in there, Agnes? Where's my tea?" Ian's voice rose like a cross child's.

Where's my tea? Where are my pills? Where's my pipe?

Where's my life? Where's the little hotel we planned on those Ballachulish nights? Where are the three sons (or daughters) we wanted? Where's sex? Where's love? Where's Ian? Where am I?

Agnes took the tea and cups on a tray, along with a plate of sandwiches and shortbread, into the other room.

"I'm sorry. I was daydreaming."

"Daydreaming of what your life will be like when I'm dead?"

"Oh Ian, I wish you wouldn't talk like that."

"Why not? I'm dying. We both know that."

"We're all dying, Ian. But how you feel, how you are, affects the quality of your life right now."

"What quality? What life?" Ian jerked at the plastic, blood-filled tubing that linked him to the machine.

"Yes, it's living. Without it you'd die. Why do you have to fight the machine so much? We've read the same books. You know how much your state of mind affects your body. You used to be such a believer in that."

"I did, didn't I? I was so naïve back then. I really thought I could win. Win against cancer!"

"But you can win, Ian. Winning isn't living forever. You were winning even after the third brain tumor."

"This is 1989, it must be brain tumor #3. Bloody ridiculous, isn't it? Have you ever watched those student nurses when I give my history? I always thought we should have made a tape."

This is the updated medical history of Ian McPherson.

Born 1955. Normal childhood, despite mother. Educated Dunfermline High School and Glasgow Polytechnic, electrical engineer.

1980: married Agnes Feinstein ("A Jewess, Ian?"). Life dream to make a bit of money and buy a wee hotel somewhere on the West Coast of Scotland.

1982: cancerous tumor in one kidney. Removed. Prognosis excellent. No treatment.

*1984: cancerous brain tumor. Totally encapsulated, prognosis excellent. Radiation and chemo just to make doubly sure.
1985: same blinding headaches. Suspected tumor.
Operation. Only scar tissue.
1986: second brain tumor, same place, same kind.
1988: cancerous tumor in kidney #2—too big to remove partially. Home dialysis. Cozy little unit set up in the corner of our dream hotel. Ian doing the books and ordering the groceries on the phone while the wonder machine does its work.
1989: brain tumor #3. "We got **most** of it, Ian"
1989: various metastases in the lungs. Inoperable. Silence.*

"Silence. High-priced, professional silence." Ian's voice was bitter. "Only the sound of the doctor rustling papers on his desk, the nurses bustling with the bedpans, you cooking up a storm in the kitchen, the doorbell ringing with deliveries of flowers, cards, casseroles, but never any people. At least, up here, people have an excuse. I have an excuse for them not to visit."

"People don't know what to say, or do, Ian. They want to help, but they don't know how."

"I don't know how anymore either, Agnes." Ian lifted his wrist, the wrist that wasn't laden with tubing and needles and peered at his watch. "Is it not time yet? I've had enough of this damn machine for one day. Fifteen more minutes. I can't wait that long. I've got to get off now."

He started grabbing Kelly clamps off the top of the machine and clamping tubes off at various points.

"It's only fifteen more minutes, Ian. You need the full run."

"You always used to say if something isn't going to matter in five years time, then it's not worth worrying about. This certainly isn't going to matter in one year, let alone five. Are you going to help me, or shall I do it myself?"

Five minutes later Ian was unhooked from the machine

and pacing up and down in front of the window, one hand holding a cotton swab pressed to the puncture in his arm. He wore a pair of drawstring corduroy pants and big sweater, both of which hung loosely on his thin frame. He was completely bald, apart from some grey fuzz at the back of his head and around his ears. A large, purplish scar like a clown's eyebrow and a three day stubble were the only color on his greying skin.

Frowning and breathing heavily, Agnes wrenched the contaminated tubing off the machine and bundled it into a plastic bag.

*Even my mother doesn't come. I can understand and forgive all the others. I don't even care about Ian's mother. She just makes it worse. But my mother. She'll be marvelous when he's gone. She's got it all planned out. But it'll be too late. She'll be marvellous as mother-of-the-widow, but **this** isn't a reality she can comprehend.*

This was Agnes' reality. Tubes lately vacated by Ian's blood and distilled water. A large container of Ian's urine newly flushed out of his body. Stacks of boxes containing the supplies for the next few weeks—tubing, needles, clamps, medication, gauze, tape. Four and a half hours on the machine three times a week, an hour of set-up and an hour of clean-up each time, special meals to be made and coaxed into him, ten different kinds of pills at different times of the day and night. Interferon injections three times a week. Every two weeks a day trip to Glasgow to see the doctor and have lunch with Mother.

Which did I dread the most? It was like being taken out from boarding school as a child. I was dying to confide in any caring soul that Maggie Currie was now best friends with Jessie Lambert and that I had to walk to church on Sundays with Rosie Lawson who smelled. But all Mother talked about was her recent cruise down the Nile.

"The rain's stopped, Agnes. I think I'll go out for a bit of a walk."

"Why don't you have a rest, Ian, and go later. You're always so cold and tired after the run."

"For Christ's sake, Agnes. One day you nag me for lying around and sleeping too much. Now you're trying to make me go to bed. I feel like going out, that's all."

"I'll come with you, then."

"I don't need a babysitter, Agnes."

"I know you don't, Ian. I'd like to come with you."

"Well, I don't feel like any company, thank you."

Agnes turned and went to the cupboard and brought Ian a pair of thick socks, his black Wellington boots and oilskin jacket. She knelt to help him put on his socks. Ian accepted passively, leaning back in the chair, his eyes closed.

Such an effort, just getting dressed, and as soon as I begin to walk to the door the hips begin to hurt again. "Every drug has a side effect." I could write a book on that one. I'm a walking casebook on side effects.

It was cold outside. The rain had stopped completely and a weak sun shone through the clouds. The lighthouse on the point was clearly visible through the thinning mist. The peaks of Mora, one with a dusting of snow, shimmered above the clouds. A fierce wind flattened the dun grass.

This was their first spring in the little house in Port Appin. They were renting by the month. Up until last summer they had lived in Glasgow. Ian had a job at Marconi, a big electronics factory. Agnes ran her own catering company. Every penny they made was salted away for the dream hotel—the dream that now would never be realized. Weekends they'would drive up the West Coast in their Ford Escort walking and looking, planning and dreaming. Two weeks in the summer they rented this cottage. Whose idea had it been to come here permanently? Had it been a good idea?

Secretly they both thought that Ian wouldn't last the winter. Hell, Ian hadn't wanted to last the winter. But here it was

March, and he was still here.

The seal's out there again. I can't see her, but I know she's there. Those big eyes. Are they trusting? Are they pleading? She reminds me of Agnes. Agnes then, not Agnes now. Agnes the summer we went to Yugoslavia, Budva. We went to make a baby. God, we tried. But we didn't know that trying wasn't the problem. Agnes's skin turned a pale golden color, her hair was long and streamed back from her face when she swam up from the depths, eyes dark and inviting. Her limbs smooth and round, always a sheen of suntan oil. Everything a prelude to sex. The plump round olives, the denuded pits caressed on the tongue, the rocks hot from the midday sun on buttocks and thighs, the bloodwarm waves licking at your skin. Do you remember, Agnes? Do you remember? Sitting in a waist-deep pool in a secluded bay, your breasts bobbing on the waves, my limply satisfied sex adorned with seaweed. Why did that go too? My hair, my kidneys, my hips, my sex, my life, all ebbing away. And with it, our dreams, our love, our voices.

Agnes turned the dialysis machine to flush, and poured herself a large Scotch and sat on the window seat sipping it slowly. The light was beginning to fade and the lights from the machine were reflected in the window as it went through its automatic cycle of clean, rinse, flush and disinfect.

God, I hate that machine. Were we naïve, gullible, inflexible? We were so positive. I was so positive. The only thing I can be positive about now is my future, when he dies. And I hope it comes soon. There, I've said it. And I mean it. This isn't a life. It's not a life for Ian. If he's lucky he has one not-so-bad day in three. Dialysis day he feels terrible in the morning and exhausted in the evening. The day after he feels better, the next day the poison starts to build up again. The next day is D-day again. Then there are the headaches, the coughing, the heartburn, the diarrhea. Inability to concentrate, to think, to read, to focus. All he can do is lie and watch his mind and body waste away while his wife grows fatter and more distant.

And my life! Nurse, mother, teacher, torturer. Not wife, not lover, not friend. Not possible anymore. I still want my hotel. I want a strong, whole man with a broad back and flesh and muscles I can feel under my fingers. I want a penis thick with life. We're a joke the two of us. I took him into the shower with me to give him a good wash last week. When I came out I caught sight of the two of us. Me, large and pink with heat, him shivering already, his bones shining through translucent skin, his sex sad and shriveled and ashamed.

Agnes looked out of the window to where her husband was sitting on a rock at the water's edge. Beyond him on the rock she saw the seal. She had seen that same seal. Was it perhaps a silkie? Mrs. Erickson, their neighbor, was a great one for the old tales of the Western Highlands.

One of Agnes's favorites was the one about the lighthouse keeper who lived on the mainland with his wife and two children. Every four months, he used to go out to his lighthouse and stay there all alone for three months. One time, he found a poor wee seal lying on the rocks at the foot of the lighthouse. The lighthouse keeper didn't know whether she had been washed onto the rocks by a big wave, or whether she was sick from something else. But she needed care. So he took her up into the lighthouse and treated her like one of his own daughters. He laid her on his bed and wrapped her in a blanket and heated up a wee bit of his condensed milk and fed it to her.

After a few days the seal was well enough to leave the bed and flap around on the stone floors of the lighthouse. She made a flapping, swishing sound with her flippers so the lighthouse keeper called her Flippy and came to love her as he would a faithful pet. In the long, lonely evenings the two would sit and he would throw his slippers for her to fetch. When the lighthouse keeper's wife packed his bags she put in three slippers by mistake, and Flippy would line all three of them up at the foot of his little bed.

The day came when Flippy was completely better and the lighthouse keeper could see that she was longing for something. It was time for her to go back to the sea, to her own people. Huffing and puffing, he carried her, down the spiral lighthouse stair, and across the slippery rocks where he put her down in the water. Flippy swam around in a big circle, did a couple of dives, rose once and stared back at the lighthouse keeper, and then, she was gone.

A couple of days later when the lighthouse keeper was up lighting the lamps, he opened one of the windows and a freak gust of wind blew him backwards. He tumbled down the narrow spiral staircase. Three times he flipped over before he stopped. Everything hurt, and he knew that he couldn't last on his own until the relief ship came out.

He didn't even have the strength to crawl down the stairs for a dram, or to his bed. He just lay there, half-conscious. Then he heard a familiar flip-flap, flip-flap. *I must be delirious*, he thought. When he opened his eyes there was no Flippy. Instead he looked into the dark grey eyes of a tall, slim woman. Now he knew he was dreaming.

"Come, you're hurt. I'll help you," she said. And she supported him down the stairs to his bed. She took off his boots and sweater and bathed his head in cool sea water. She looked at his arm, which he knew must be broken and she splinted it and wrapped it tightly in seaweed. She brought him a strange smelling hot drink which she had made. "Drink this, it will make you feel better."

All the time he stared at this beautiful young woman, dressed in a tight-fitting dress of smooth, shiny material. Long dark hair streamed down her back. Before he could ask her who she was he fell asleep. He slept for two days and two nights and when he awoke he felt so much better. His head no longer hurt and his arm, although weak, was on the mend. He looked everywhere for the beautiful young woman. She had even left a pot of her strength-giving drink on the stove in the kitchen, so he knew he hadn't imagined her. The lighthouse keeper sat down on his bed and put his head in his hands. She was gone. It was then that he noticed his slippers, all three of them in a neat row by the side of his bed.

Agnes asked Mrs. Erickson if she had ever seen a silkie, but she replied that silkies only come to people who really need them.

_____

The wind had dropped completely now, and the sun was sinking fast behind the hills of Mora. As Ian sat on the shore, he saw his seal slither down the rocks and plop quietly into the water. She swam towards the shore, then paused, her head a dark shadow, her wake streaming like hair. She turned and swam slowly along the beach. Ian got up, with difficulty. His hips hurt like hell, and each breath in the cool evening air was a chore. Despite the chill he felt hot. He took off the knitted hat that Agnes always made him wear, and pulled out the tartan scarf that his mother had given him for Christmas. The soft, damp air felt good on his bare skin.

The tide was on its way out. The beach was part sand, part rocks, with darkening pools of water. Ian sat on one of the rocks and took off his Wellington boots and wool socks. The sand felt soft and soothing between his toes, the water gentle and healing. He bent down and scooped some water up with his palms and emptied it over his head. Gently he massaged it into his scar. The water ran down into his collar so he threw off his jacket and then pulled his sweater over his head. Finally he stood up and let his trousers drop to the sand. His thin, white body gleamed like marble in the dying light.

He had walked as far as he could and stood on the point of the sand bar looking past Lismore, down Loch Linnhe and its darkening waters. His seal still swam, now just a few feet off shore, its eyes fathomless sockets in the gloom, looking right into Ian's eyes, then turning to stare down the loch.

From the window of the cottage, Agnes watched as Ian took off his old trousers and dropped them on the sand. Her hand went to her mouth and she turned to run to the door. But she didn't. Instead she shouted through the window. "Ian! Ian! Stop! Stay!" The heavy glass and the wind snatched her useless words. Mirrored in the window, she saw her own gaping mouth and imploring eyes, as countless doctors had observed over the past years. She watched as Ian waded into the water up to his waist. She fell silent as he paused to splash water onto his arms. She gasped as he sank into the water and began to swim.

"Take care of him, Silkie. He's my Ian, too—always will be. Take good care of him."

As Agnes watched, the sun came out from behind a cloud and a weak shaft of sunlight lit up the two swimming heads — Ian's and the seal's. Then it faded and the water turned dark and still.

Stand By Your Man

I am the kind of woman
Who always stands by her man
Stands up for her man
Even stands up to her man
But when or where
Did his stand become mine?

In my twenties
The idea of being adrift
On uncharted seas
Sailing
On the winds of whim
Adventure
Chance
Seemed romantic

My thirties
A blur of frontier survival
A new country
A new career
Three new lives
Tugging at my time
Sails full
Decks abustle

The forties
Mid-life mismanagement
Career dislocation
Relocation
A house, but not a home
In every port

Gone the years of Band-Aids on knees
Now I salve lonely teenagers' hearts
Pump enthusiasm into Saturday nights at home with Mum and
Dad
Quell an octogenarian's nightmares—over the phone

One day soon
My parents will be dead and buried in another country
My children will leave
And go back to where they came from
And I will still be here
Alone
Empty
Adrift
Sheltered from the winds
By a wall of my own making
Bobbing in the scum of some small harbor
Watching from afar
My daughters
Stand by their men
As I have taught them.

Homeless

Someone else's car in the driveway
Someone else's kids climbing Malcolm's tree
While I stay in a neighbor's spare room
And eat a dozen farewell dinners

Driving across the prairies
Possessions piled in the back of the car
That for now is home
The kilometers (or should I call them miles again)
Slide by in tune with Gilbert and Sullivan
"For in spite of all temptations
To belong to other nations
He remains an Henglishman
He remains an Henglishman."
I listen to *Rumpole of the Bailey*,
k.d. lang,
Julio Iglesesias,
Bach,
Eric Clapton
An eclectic mix
Or cultural confusion?

Patsy Cline's hurtin' music
Appropriate for a sun-drenched Saskatchewan bleeding into
North Dakota
Dusty combine harvesters drone persistently across
symmetrical fields
For tomorrow may be winter
This benign landscape transformed into monochrome
Horizontal cold whistling through flesh

If I had been born a hundred years ago...
That could be me
Clutching my life in a carpet bag
Watching the train steam into the distance
While the cold bites through my European woolies
And the man I followed is not here to meet me
And the railway station is only a shack
And the land is so flat and white and endless
And my mother is five thousand miles away

Instead I purr across the prairies
Cocooned in air-conditioned, stereo comfort
Friends
Family
The law
The tow truck
A cellular phone call away

I did/didn't want to leave
I do/don't want to arrive
Beethoven's Ninth ... again
And again
And again.

But Does it Sell?

The unfamiliar ring of the new telephone startled Heather and she almost sliced herself with the knife she was using to cut into another packing case. *Who could that be?* She didn't know anyone in Houston and Ian rarely called from work. She found the phone with its high-pitched *American* ring under a pile of towels that she had unpacked that morning.

"Hello?" she said cautiously.

"Oh—I can hear that darling accent! Say something else."

"Um, this is Heather Pearson—who is this? Perhaps you have the wrong..."

"I'm sorry! How rude! This is Ruth Ann Brainerd."

"Ruth Ann Brainerd?" *Who the hell is Ruth Ann Brainerd?*

"Ruth Ann—Stan's wife."

Stan?

"Stan Brainerd, your husband's new boss," the voice, edged with impatience, continued.

Oh Christ!

"I'm sorry," Heather stuttered. "I'm knee deep in packing cases and I'm afraid my mind seems to have turned to soggy cardboard too."

"Don't apologize, honey. You don't have to tell me about the horrors of moving—thirteen moves in twenty-seven years."

Thirteen moves in ...

"And I'm phoning to rescue you from the packing cases. Can you be ready in twenty minutes?

"Twenty minutes?"

"I've lined up a bunch of the girls who are just wild to meet you—and on the way back I'll give you the guided tour."

"That's very kind, but I'm kind of busy..."

"The packing cases'll still be there tomorrow, honey—a

gal's gotta have some fun."

"But I'm a mess and I haven't unpacked any decent clothes."

"All these women have moved many times, Heather—just come as you are—this is real casual. Tell you what, I'll give you an extra half hour. I'll pick you up at—ten after twelve. Don't worry—we're real casual here. See you then. Byeee!"

"Ruth Ann—I—Ruth Ann..."

Shit! She's gone! The last thing Heather wanted to do was go out and socialize. She caught a glimpse of herself in the big mirror she had just unpacked. Streaky blond hair that needed to be touched up and cut—she just hadn't had time the last little while. An okay face, square, relatively wrinkle free, the kind of face that looked better without make-up, a body that definitely needed some work—two months of fast food and Rufus' death had taken their toll—walking without Rufus's tail waving ahead of her as he snuffled through the grass was no fun.

Oh well! she sighed. She didn't know the woman's telephone number. She might as well go take a shower.

Half an hour later when the door bell rang, she was, at least, clean. She thought she looked presentable, dressed in cord pants and one of Ian's white shirts—better than she had for the past week or so.

Heather opened the front door to a cloud of expensive perfume. A tall, pencil thin woman with a cap of professionally tinted blond hair thrust out both her hands.

"Heather! Welcome to Houston!"

Ruth Ann leaned forward and grasped both of Heather's hands in hers. Heather could feel Ruth Ann's long red finger nails and several large rings. When she pulled back, Heather noticed that Ruth Ann was wearing a pair of tapered, chocolate leather pants and a long taupe mohair tunic. She looked down at her own cord pants and white shirt.

"Are we ready then?" asked Ruth Ann.

"'fraid so," apologized Heather. "I knew that even if I did find something smarter, I'd never be able to find the iron!"

"Don't worry! You look fine." Ruth Ann inspected Heather's jeans. "We're meeting the others at the club—very casual."

Three other women were waiting at the Houston Golf and Country Club, in the Grill Room. "I know you're into casual, Heather, so I changed our reservation from the dining room," Ruth Ann explained as she guided Heather to the white-clothed table by the window. Heather was glad to see that two of the women were dressed as though they had just come off the golf course. The third woman was something else—huge—in an expensive New York copy of an African tribal caftan, oversize rings on every finger and a brick red turban.

"This flamboyant creature is Rebecca Steiner," explained Ruth Ann. "Her significant other, Irving, **Senator** Steiner, is our local bigwig. And Becky is the brains and brawn behind Fine & Stein."

"The poor gal's probably still climbing out of the packing cases, Ruthie," interrupted one of the golfers. "Fine & Stein, Houston's **finest,** Houston's **only** art gallery. Becky's got a real nose for art. Sold me a Michael Moser way back when and now it's worth five thou! I'm Betty Lou Daugherty, by the way."

"Another selfless supporter of the Arts," Ruth Ann interjected. "Betty Lou is the perennial president of our Symphony Board and tireless board member and volunteer in God knows how many other organizations."

"Do you work, Heather?"

The second golfer shrieked, "She's at it already. Get your excuses ready, Heather. Betty Lou recruits volunteers in her sleep!" She stuck out her hand. "I'm Lauralyn Plotsky. Good to have you here."

Betty Lou snorted. "You certainly can't talk, Laurie. I pamper my volunteers and anyway, I asked first."

"Lauralyn is a fund-raising consultant, known state-wide for her ability to get blood out of stones," explained Ruth Ann.

"Or funds out of old man Steiner," interrupted Betty Lou.

"My father-in-law was not known for his generosity," said Rebecca. "But Laurie hounded him till he cracked."

"Well, do you work, Heather?"persisted Betty Lou.

"No," answered Heather. "I can't work here until I get a green card."

"Well, don't worry," continued Betty Lou. "We'll keep you plenty busy—a great way to make new friends, too."

"I'm kind of looking forward to not working. I've dabbled in writing and I hope to be able to spend some more time doing that."

Lauralyn shrieked again."Can you believe that? She's a writer, Ruth Ann. Isn't that wild?"

"What do you write, honey?" asked Ruth Ann, while the other three sat on the edge of their chairs.

Heather couldn't understand what the fuss was about, but she answered anyway. "A bit of this, a bit of that. I used to have my own little business back home—did contract writing—brochures, articles, that sort of thing."

"Interesting," said Betty Lou.

"And I've always dabbled in other writing—short stories, a bit of poetry—I've even tried my hand at a novel and a screenplay." Heather always felt embarrassed admitting to writing. It was almost as bad as playing bingo every afternoon.

"And have you published anything?" asked Lauralyn.

"A few poems here, the occasional short story there—in little literary magazines that only other writers read." Heather laughed. *Why were the three women exchanging glances like that?*

"Tell her, Ruthie," Betty Lou urged.

Ruth Ann just smiled.

"Well, if you don't, I will," said Lauralyn. "You've really lucked out, Heather. Meet our local literary celebrity." She gestured to Ruth Ann. "Ta da!"

"Literary celebrity is pushing it, Laurie," smiled Ruth Ann. "But I do write and I can't tell you how thrilled I am to have another writer in our little group."

"I'll lend you Ruthie's book of poems and anecdotes and you can rent her movie at the local movie store," said Betty Lou.

"Wow ! I'm impressed—and intimidated," said Heather.

Ruth Ann smiled.

The conversation turned to other topics—many other topics. These women had, it seemed, an expert opinion on almost anything one could talk about. But it was nice to get away from the packing cases and just sit, eat, smile and let it all wash over her. Heather had to admit that they were very friendly and kind, offering all sorts of advice on "cute" doctors, "hunky" dentists, the only place in town to have your hair done, but "don't tell him your secrets, honey, or the whole town'll know!" Heather really wanted to go home after the lunch but Ruth Ann wouldn't hear of it. "I've blocked off the whole afternoon. Don't worry about dinner—we'll wheel by Pasta Presto on the way home—a great standby for busy gals like us!"

Ruth Ann even had a pad and pencil at the ready for Heather to jot down the names and addresses of the "only decent butcher" in town, Ruth Ann's clever little seamstress, the funky little flower shop run by Ruth Ann's "hippie" sister-in-law.

It was only on the way home that the subject of writing came up again. "Let me give you a little friendly advice, honey, about the local writing scene," Ruth Ann began. "They're an odd bunch. If I were you I'd stay well clear of them."

"I thought I might try and get into a writing group," said Heather, "you know, meet with some other writers who might spur me on to actually finishing something."

"Good idea. I'll take you out to my writing group in Ichiwana. Whatever you do, don't join any of the groups in town."

"Why not?"

"Politics, honey—politics. The writing scene here is controlled by this self-made guru of poetry, Paddy Illikainan—weedy little man who plays the part of the starving poet eking out a miserable existence in his garret—can't stand the idea that there might be regular people—middle-class (shudder) even WEALTHY people out there who can actually write. No, our little group in Ichiiwana is the place for you! Real people—country people—mixed bag, of course, but that's what it's all about."

"But isn't Ichiiwana way out of town?"

"It's less than an hour's drive—makes for a nice day. We do lunch after our meeting. We won't be meeting next week but I'll call you the following week and we can go out together."

"I don't know that..."

"Tell me about your screenplay—now **that** whole scene is a viper's nest. I hate to say this, but I sure hope you're having fun writing it because selling it or getting it made is a real long shot."

"So how did yours get made then?" Heather was beginning to feel a little irritated.

"I was **asked** to write the screenplay. I'd been publishing animal stories for a year or so, and a producer asked me to develop the screenplay."

"That must have been fun."

"Hell, it wasn't. It was a major pain. Is your screenplay finished—and what's it about?"

"Well, yes—I've done a couple of drafts." Heather hated talking about her writing. It always sounded so pathetic and she was painfully aware of the fact that she had spent most of her adult life writing, but had very little to show for it.

"It's a comedy—a very silly comedy—no redeeming intellectual features!" She gave a little embarrassed laugh.

"A comedy—as in a full-length feature?" asked Ruth Ann.

"That makes it sound awfully grand," laughed Heather.

"Almost impossible to sell—on-spec comedies or dramas," declared Ruth Ann firmly. "I would try something different if I..."

"But I have had some interest," interrupted Heather. "A couple of companies from Hollywood have asked to see the next draft."

"Oh sure, they do that—no skin off their nose—I don't suppose they've offered you any money?"

"Well no, not yet."

"Probably won't—I hope you have the idea registered—if they like the idea they'll steal that off you. But the chances of a newcomer, like you, actually being paid to develop a script—that just doesn't happen, honey."

"But I've heard of quite a few people who—"

"Hollywood myth, honey. No, the reality is that Hollywood eats little people like you for breakfast."

Ruth Ann pulled into the driveway of Heather's house and although Heather was not looking forward to getting back to the packing cases, she just couldn't wait to get out of the car. She didn't know what kind of writer Ruth Ann was, but her supreme confidence was really getting to Heather.

"Thank you very much for the wonderful lunch and all the helpful information, Ruth Ann," she said as she opened the door.

Ruth Ann shrugged. "Think nothing of it sweetie. That's what friends are for. See you Friday."

"Friday? "Heather was confused. Had she missed something. "What's happening Friday?"

"Party—our place."

Heather still looked confused, so Ruth Ann continued. "You don't mean to tell me that Ian didn't tell you. Men! Honestly! They're hopeless. I'm having a little party for you and Ian—just a few of Houston's finest—everyone's dying to meet you—new blood in our little community and all."

"But I don't have anything to wear..."

"Surely you'll have finished the unpacking by then. Or else go out and buy something new. Capitalize on Ian's guilt feelings for making you move." Ruth Ann pointed to the rings on her fingers, first a large opal. "That was Chicago—this one was Detroit—and this beauty," she indicated the heavy gold bracelet, "was Venezuela —paid for every goddamn ounce of gold in that hellhole of a place!" She brayed with laughter.

Heather let herself out of the car and stood waving on the steps while Ruth Ann roared back out of the driveway and drove off with a wave of red-manicured fingers.

"I suppose we really do have to go," said Heather reluctantly as she looked at herself in the mirror. Behind her on the bed lay several discarded outfits. Her wardrobe reflected her schizophrenic personality, she thought. She rejected the silk two-piece bought when her mother was visiting—too bourgeois, the black mini sheath bought for the Christmas party the year Ian hired that gorgeous leggy engineer—too daring. She cast a critical eye over the old standby she had chosen—floaty black skirt and multi-colored shirt. She frowned at her reflection—*throwback to the Sixties.*

Ian came out of the bathroom, splotches of tissue on his face. "Are you sure you haven't seen my razor—I hate these disposable jobbies."

"I think it must have been thrown out—I'll buy you a new one tomorrow." She patted her husband on his rounded stomach. "Those little bits of tissue make you look so vulnerable— bring out my maternal instinct. Why don't you leave them on for the party—give them something to talk about?"

"Right!" Ian looked over at the clothes on the bed. "What's wrong with the black one?"

"What's wrong with this outfit?" Heather shot back.

"Nothing—but you know how much I like that black one."

Heather laughed. "You're myopic, Ian Pearson—I really

don't think you see the twenty extra pounds and God knows how many inches—I'm too fat for..."

"No, you're not—and those legs..."

Ian pressed Heather against the wall, reached under her black skirt and stroked her thigh. Heather laughed and pushed him away. "Stop it, Ian! We'll never get to the party—not that I wouldn't mind—but if it makes you feel better, I'll wear the black dress. Dig in that box over there and find me a pair of black tights without runs in them..."

Ian ran to the half-emptied packing box on the other side of the bed and buried his head inside it, snuffling like a happy puppy. "Black stockings with runs in them—oooh—heaven!"

The Brainerds lived in a large, Spanish-style house with red tiled roof, wrought iron shutters, wrap-around red tile patio crowded with ornate clay planters stuffed with brightly-colored flowers. People were already clustered on the patio. It seemed as though conversation stopped and they all turned to watch Heather try to get out of the car without tripping over the curb.

Ruth Ann, on the arm of a large, aggressively good-looking man, came down the steps smiling broadly. Ruth Ann, first glancing at her husband, withdrew her hand and stretched out both arms. "Dear people—welcome to our home—welcome to our community!" Ruth Ann looked at her husband again and he gave an almost imperceptible nod and led everyone into applause. Heather didn't quite know what to do. Curtsy? A royal wave? She smiled through her panic. Thank God, Ian rose to the occasion. Holding his hand up to quiet the applause, he spoke. "Thank you, thank you all. And thank you Ruth Ann and Stan. Heather and I are really glad to be here in Houston and we look forward to meeting you all—or should I say y'all!" That brought a burst of laugher and more applause, and then Heather was whisked away to meet a succession of golf-course tanned men and even-toothed women who all smiled and touched and, of course, exclaimed about her "cute accent."

Ruth Ann was the perfect hostess. She was dressed in what would have looked like a pair of pajamas on Heather—a simple black silk pantsuit—with several heavy gold chains around her neck and wrist and enormous dangling earrings. She looked great. But she was different today—nervous, distracted. She darted like a bird trapped in a room—from Heather, to the kitchen, back bearing trays of canapés, to Stan's side, to the bar to point out guests with empty glasses to the black-suited waiters.

Heather was in conversation with a small blond woman who was talking about golf. "Ya mean to tell me y're from Scotland and ya don't golf?"

Heather smiled apologetically, "Sorry! I tried it once and was just terrible—it takes so long too!"

"Well, you gotta golf here, honey. Ya won't see your man, if ya don't golf. That's all they do—work and golf—at least if you're lucky, that's all they do!" She laughed, showing perfect, even, pearly white teeth. "Ron," she looked around the room and caught the eye of a short balding man in a white leisure suit. "He's a keeper, that one. Third time lucky, I guess. He's crazy for golf. Not that I can really play with him—I don't even have a handicap. But it gives us something to talk about over cocktails. You gotta join our Tuesday Morning Ladies' Group—we have a blast!"

"Well, I..." Heather was just starting to make excuses when she felt a hand on her arm. She turned and there was Stan. "You gotta excuse us Barbie. I'm going to monopolize our guest of honor for a while."

Barbie smiled and patted Stan on his tanned hand. "Fine with me, Stannie—it's your party!"

Stan took Heather's arm and tucked it into his own. "This is just an excuse, I know, but I want a chance to get you on your own. I want to show you my mother's coat-of-arms. Did Ian tell you that my mother was a Paterson—fiercely proud of her Scottish heritage—made me learn the bagpipes and Highland dancing when I was a kid." Stan laughed. *Do they all have perfect teeth here? Must be some rich dentists.* "You'll have to join our Houston Scottish Heritage Association. The Burns Dinner at the Windsor Club is the highlight of the social year!"

By this time, they were in what Heather assumed was Stan's study. A cozy room with dark wood and plaid wallpaper, plaid upholstery on the single large armchair, a huge leather-topped desk, expensive stereo system, giant screen TV. "My aerie," explained Stan. "I've always needed a place to be on my own, time to reflect." He was still holding Heather's arm and he spun her around and stared into her eyes. "I get the feeling you're that kind of person." Heather lowered her eyes under his eagle stare. "Well, yes—I suppose."

"Ruth Ann's the complete opposite," he interrupted. "Can't stand to be on her own—always twittering on the telephone to one pal or another."

"But she's a writer—she must need..." said Heather.

"Pphh! Ruth Ann's writing! Don't get me started on that subject!" Stan gestured over his shoulder to a framed coat of arms hanging above his desk. "There's the coat of arms. My mother and I went back the year before she died and poked around in old graveyards."

"She must have really appreciated that," said Heather.

"Yeah, the old duck loved it. Visited every goddamned cemetery in the country—never want to see another tombstone 'til it's mine!"

Heather smiled weakly, and Stan went on. "But I really spirited you away up here to..."

Oh God, he's going to come on to me!

"To tell you how glad I am to have Ian and you in town," Stan continued. "Your ol' man's pretty hot property, ya know. We're damned pleased with ourselves that we won him away from the competition."

Heather smiled, genuinely this time. It's always good to

hear friends and family praised, and Ian deserved it. "And I of all people know," Stan went on, "the importance of the li'l woman behind the scenes! You go through the CEOs of the Fortune 500 Companies—they're pretty well all married, many of them still on their first wives—definite asset."

Heather's smile dimmed somewhat. "You're obviously speaking from experience. Ruth Ann is just wonderful—and she's an acclaimed writer as well."

Stan frowned. "Yeah, she does try very hard. She'd be better off working on her golf swing than her writing, though."

Heather gasped. "How can you say that? She's published books, given readings, even sold a screenplay that has actually been made into a movie."

"Well yeah—but there's publishing and publishing—her best friend's second cousin Lowell who runs a small press out of the basement of his farm isn't exactly Bantam Books! Is it Ruth?" he boomed as the door opened and she came in.

"No, Stan, it's not," said Ruth Ann in a small, sad voice. She'd heard this statement before, Heather thought. She had applied fresh make-up and the red slash of her mouth looked like a gaping wound in her tight, white face. Her hands fluttered nervously. "I was wondering where you had gone. Lots of people still want to meet Heather, you know."

"The pitch of your voice is rising, Ruth," said Stan quietly. "You know how I feel about that."

Ruth Ann coughed. With her hand to her throat and, after a couple of false starts, she spoke in a low voice, "I'm sorry, honey, I just..."

"Never mind—we're coming," Stan interrupted. "Ready to face the hordes, Heather?"

"Absolutely!" said Heather, and turned to Ruth Ann. "Stan was just telling me about your trip to Scotland with his mother, where you visited every cemetery between Gretna Green and John O'Groats."

"Right," said Ruth Ann almost under her breath. "I visited every wind-blasted cemetery, while **Stan** and his cronies played every golf course."

"You're exaggerating, Sugar—as usual," said Stan quietly, as he swept Heather out of the room and back down to the party.

After another hour of small talk Heather's smile was as brittle as a sun-dried sand dollar and she had to fight back the urge to trot out a sample of Glasgow gutter language if asked again to demonstrate her "peachy accent." She excused herself and went to look for Ian. She finally spotted him on the deck behind a huge pot of the biggest pansies she'd ever seen, talking to Stan.

Heather sidled up the side of the porch, trying to avoid getting embroiled in any other conversations. As she reached the plant, she overheard Ian say, "Heather's written a screenplay too." She froze. Much as she loved Ian and as close as they were, she had never really shared her writing with him. He was such a strong personality and she had been so taken over, quite voluntarily, into his way of life, that she protected the privacy of her writing as some last bastion of her individuality. She was diffident about her writing too. Perhaps Ian thought it was all a bit of a waste of time, but was too nice a person ever to tell her.

She was about to sneak back and approach them more publicly when she heard Stan respond. "Now there's an area to keep well clear of. Whatever you do, Ian, don't do what I did."

"What do you mean?" Ian asked, puzzled.

"I kind of went along with Ruth Ann's writing thing. After all, a gal's gotta have something to do and it seemed harmless enough. She'd been writing these sappy little animal stories which she was pretty pleased about and she had them published by some hokey little press—didn't cost too much—I thought it was worth it—made her happy—at the time I was kind of busy."

Stan paused and laughed unpleasantly. Heather could

hardly see them but she could hear the naïve confusion in Ian's voice. "What do you mean, busy?"

"Quit kidding, Ian," roared Stan. "You know just what I mean—working **late** at the office, **emergency** business trips. Well the shit hit the fan one day when Ruth Ann found some black panties in my suit coat pocket."

Heather strained to see Ian's reaction to that. As usual, when embarrassed, he looked as though he had a plum in each cheek. "That was the same time that Ruth Ann was approached to use one of her furry animal ideas for a movie," continued Stan. "Anyway, before I knew where I was, I'd come up with fifty grand to make 'he movie on the understanding that Ruth Ann would get the screenplay."

"Fifty grand, eh?" whistled Ian.

"Yeah—expensive little fuck, wasn't it," laughed Stan. "It was billed as an investment, but, needless to say, I haven't seen a dime."

"Well, it must have made Ruth Ann happy," said Ian.

"I don't even know about that. She got royally screwed around with the script. I guess the finished product stinks—**I** never watched it. And, come to think of it, I don't even know if Ruth Ann still writes. She never mentions it. But you know what it's like—if it keeps them out of your hair, eh Ian?"

Ian cleared his throat. "Actually, I've always been very proud of Heather's writing—and more than a little envious. I'm the classic illiterate engineer—mind just doesn't work like that." He laughed. "Heather's pretty private about her writing, but I've gone into her files on the computer to read some of her stuff and I think it's pretty damn good."

"But does it sell? That's the point, isn't it?"

"I used to think that was the point," continued Ian. "I was forever pushing Heather to be more popular, get an agent, study the markets—but now I don't know. Now, I kind of think it's enough that her friends, the children and I—and perhaps their children, will read it."

Stan sounded disappointed. "You're a more patient man than me, for sure."

They started to move away. Heather, swallowing the lump in her throat, pushed round the large pot. "There you are," she said, feigning surprise. She went up and put her arm through Ian's. "I think it's time we tear ourselves away from this wonderful party."

Ian tucked her hand into his. "Have you been running, you sound kind of out of breath?" he asked. "No, no nothing like that," replied Heather squeezing his hand. "You still take her breath away, you dirty dog," laughed Stan. "You lucky dog," he added.

They found Ruth Ann by the door saying good-bye to some other guests. Ian stuck his hand out, "Wonderful party, Ruth Ann."

"You think so?" replied Ruth Ann, looking at Stan. "Stan's got very fixed ideas about a successful party. Everything, just everything, has to be perfect."

She looked at Stan again, but he had moved away to talk to some other people. "Well, it was," said Heather, and she gave Ruth Ann a big hug. "It was a perfect party. You'll have to give me some tips. And you are perfect too. I can't thank you enough for all your help and advice. This move would have been perfectly beastly without a friend like you. I hope I can call you a friend."

Heather knew she was laying it on a bit thick, exaggerating the accent.She made a point of not looking at Ian as she knew he would have that bemused expression on his face.

"Of course, you can call me your friend," beamed Ruth Ann. "I'm just glad I could help."

"And we'll have to meet next week and you can give me the lowdown on the local literary scene," continued Heather.

"Sure, honey," purred Ruth Ann. "I'd love to do that. And I'd love to see your screenplay."

"Anytime," said Heather, as she went down the steps,

waving over her shoulder.

As they drove off Ian remarked, laughing, "What was that all about?"

"Oh, nothing," replied Heather with a little smile. And she slid over the bench seat and put her head on Ian's shoulder and tucked her hand between his legs. "Let's go home."

The Retirement Party

For once, Martha thoroughly agreed with what the Company was doing. She told everyone that she wasn't going along with this new retirement policy because it was what Jack wanted. She knew it looked like that. All in all, the Company had been good to them both. She owed them a retirement party, she supposed. She'd been to more than her share of them, and this one promised to be no different. Everybody and their "spouse"—the Company was very proud of the fact that they made such an effort to make the spouses feel included—dressed in their best to bid farewell to a familiar, but little-known colleague. Even the clothes hadn't changed much over the years. The only thing that distinguished them from the rest of the party was that she had the statutory corsage and Jack had a pink rosebud in his lapel.

"A drink, Marty?" Martha turned to see Jack with two glasses filled with a pink, fizzy drink. "The maître d' made these specially for us."

"You know that I'm not big on cocktails, Jack."

"I know, honey, but he was most insistent—I think we should drink it."

"Do you think there's anything...?"

"Just drink it. I'm sure it's fine."

The drink tasted unusual, but not unpleasant, and after she finished, Jack led her to the head table. It was a long table on a raised dais, set only on one side so they could look down over the rest of the party. That was the only good thing about these retirement dinners—being able to sit and watch everyone. She had to admit that this was a pretty lavish affair. They had overdone the flowers though—that was tactless.

Jack seemed to be enjoying himself. She had always envied him his ease with people. She knew she had a reputation for being aloof, certainly among the women. She was always pleasant if someone spoke to her, but it was a duty.

She was glad to see Sandy MacLean from Personnel sit down on her right. He was one of her few friends in the Company. He didn't look his usual cheery self tonight. Jack had told her that he was one of two board members who hadn't voted in favor of the New Retirement Policy. For once, he seemed at a loss for words. Martha was still doing all the talking when a fat hand with a large diamond signet ring covered hers.

"Martha, dear—you look wonderful." George Smart's standard greeting to all female spouses—*what was his greeting to male spouses*, she wondered. Unlike Sandy, George was beaming from ear to ear. And so he should be. Jack's retirement opened the way for him; as of tomorrow he would be the new president.

His wife Barbie—**another** *new dress*, Martha noted, baby blue angora to match her eyes—leaned forward from beyond him and spoke in that awful nasal twang. "We're all going to miss you so much, Marthy."

Like hell, Martha thought—Barbie had been preparing for the role of President's wife all her married life. She would certainly be popular with the other presidents and chairmen and their wives. She would sign up for every excursion on the Ladies' Conference Program and make a point of being in the front row for the quasi-business sessions which these conferences now offered as pap to the New Woman. Martha always hated conferences. They reminded her of boarding school, always doing things in a group, always having to try to be bright, witty, fun. Barbie loved that kind of thing. After all, she and George paid to go on cruises and guided bus tours to the Pyramids for their vacations.

George had moved to the podium. He tapped the microphone to get everyone's attention.

"Would you all please stand?"

Chairs scraped back and everyone stood with bowed heads, some even folded their hands. "We thank you, Maker, for the food we are about to share with our dear, departing friends, Martha and Jack."

Over the years, government policy regarding religious practices had become more invasive—all in the name of tolerance, of course. They had recently issued a booklet of graces, prayers, thanksgivings to be used in groups where there was the slightest possibility there might be more than one religion represented. This protocol had taken umpteen years, millions of dollars and a lot of anguish to produce. The result was so wishy-washy that it appealed to no one.

Martha picked up the gold-embossed menu; their names *Jack & Martha* were printed on the front in fancy calligraphic print. It was a very grand menu, not the standard four-shrimp shrimp cocktail and overdone Cornish game hen. It included most of their favorite foods—smoked salmon, artichoke soup, rack of lamb—even leeks, and a different wine with every course. She turned to Sandy. "This looks like your doing!"

"We've shared enough meals over the past twenty years for me to know what your favorites are—the least I can do." Sandy smiled sadly.

"So, is this the year you're planning to take all that back vacation?" Sandy's workaholism was a company joke.

"You'll be glad to hear that I **am** taking a holiday this year. I'm off tomorrow to the northwest corner of Vancouver Island."

"Northwest Vancouver Island in November—that

sounds like **my** kind of holiday. But I know what you mean—
two weeks of wave watching a year should be compulsory.
Maybe that'll be the next thing!"

The Company had spared no expense this evening.
The food was a visual feast. But, sadly, it looked better than
it tasted. That seemed to be the norm lately. In fact, Jack
just said on the weekend that everything tasted the same.
Tomatoes were redder, cucumbers greener, meat pinker, eggs
larger, but they didn't taste as good anymore. "If you thought
about it," Jack said, "it wasn't really surprising." Food pro-
duction had been forced to undergo a radical change since
their youth. And nobody could disagree with the facts. It
was safer, more productive, more economical to grow fruit
and vegetables in greenhouses, to raise livestock in barns, to
farm fish in carefully controlled ponds—away from the haz-
ards of acid rain, nuclear spills, virus epidemics. Uniformity
of taste was the necessary price.

Martha looked along the table at Jack. He was talk-
ing to Sandy's wife, Joanne. He didn't look seventy. He didn't
look like a man attending his second retirement party. The
first one had been fifteen years ago. Back then, early retire-
ment had been all the rage. It seemed like a good idea at the
time; there was so much unemployment, especially among
the young. The government and the companies had put to-
gether some pretty tempting offers—over time, incentive
gave way to subtle pressure and finally legislation.

But it hadn't worked. They should have known what
would happen. The younger men were just not as experi-
enced. They didn't know how to work the system. The com-
puterized experience retrieval centers weren't as sophisti-
cated as today. At first, they called all the retirees back as
highly-paid consultants, but everyone knew how uneconomi-
cal that was. Ten years later, they were all back in their old

jobs. But nothing changed. The advanced technology meant more people for fewer jobs. George Smart told her she should be proud to be spearheading the program.

The swing doors to the kitchen opened and several waiters appeared wheeling dessert trolleys. Martha was most relieved to see that they had decided against a cake with candles. The first trolley stopped behind her chair. Once again, Sandy had been instrumental in choosing the desserts. Martha had a hyper-sweet tooth and this particular trolley was laden with all her favorites—chocolate eclairs, Black Forest cake, mud pie, cheesecake, profiteroles, meringues. But it didn't seem as enticing as it usually did. Half the fun of choosing a horribly rich, fattening dessert was the sublimation of guilt— and that wasn't necessary today.

The whole meal reminded her of those Sunday evening dinners at home before she had to return to boarding school on Monday morning. Delicious as those weekends were, they were always filled with a frenzy of activity designed to sustain body and soul for the next six weeks. And it all culminated in the Sunday night dinner where Mother cooked all the favorite foods, brother Paul cut down on the teasing and Father talked about topics other than the Church and his rose garden—the Last Suppers as they were irreverently called.

At least those dinners didn't have speeches. Father would usually go on a bit about developing good study habits and why she must take calculus, and Mother would murmur, almost to herself, about the importance of keeping warm below the waist and of eating one piece of fresh fruit a day.

George Smart was a short man and he had to adjust the microphone downward. He stood and beamed out over the audience, the lights reflecting off his glasses and his receding hairline.

"It really touches my heart to see so many of you here today to say good-bye to our much loved President, Jack Coleman, and his lovely wife, Martha."

George paused—he had obviously taken the course at the Sincerely Superior Speech School, and the audience filled the pause with hearty applause for the two retirees.

"It touches my heart, but it doesn't surprise me. Jack has been our President for eight years now and has deservedly gained the respect and love of us all. It was Jack Coleman who engineered the brilliant takeover of the Efficient Energy Corporation. It was Jack Coleman who spearheaded the Paperless Office Program..." George blotted his dry eyes with his hankerchief.

"And so it is typical that Jack Coleman is leading again by embracing the Company's most innovative and imaginative policy to date, namely, our New Retirement Plan."

Another pause. An even bigger round of applause. *And let us not forget in our accolades, his loyal wife without whom, blah blah..."* Martha thought.

On cue George turned to Martha. "And of course, we must not forget Martha. As you know, our Company has set the tone for industry in general with its positive attitude towards women, both as employees and as spouses. We know that a supportive spouse is an equal partner, in family **and** corporate achievements. Martha Coleman is a shining example of such a partner..."

Sure enough, George launched into praises of her loyalty, fortitude, encouragement. She supposed she did deserve them but it irked her to hear it from George. And had it all been worthwhile? What had she really done?

Oh yes, there had been the volunteer work. George was listing all that now. But how much good had she really done? What had she really accomplished? She didn't enjoy it. That was why she had tried so many different things. Of course, in George's list, her lack of enthusiasm didn't come across. It just sounded as though she had been amazingly busy helping anyone and everyone. In reality, she had only started volunteering because she felt guilty and then continued because it was too difficult to get out of.

Martha's mother was one of those people who was always giving things away to the "poor people." Every few months, she scoured the house and made up parcels of clothes, books, toys, and household equipment to take to one group or other. Every package had to contain one real "sacrifice"— an oft-read book, a favorite dress and, on one painful occasion, Baby Jane with standing-on-end hair, an ABC written on her cloth body.

George was into the, "How much we will miss them, but the benefits of their contributions and their warm memory will be with the Company forever and ever, Amen," section.

One down and one to go. Sandy looked very uncomfortable as he made his way to the podium, and Joanne looked worried. Sandy was carrying his speech carefully written out; that was unusual. He started reading.

"Not only has Jack Coleman been my colleague for the past twenty years, but he and Martha have become very close friends of ours. I would like to tell you about some of the highlights of Jack's career as I remember them."

"Would you speak a little louder," a voice called from the back of the room.

Sandy raised his voice minimally and continued. "I don't want to downplay his corporate successes, but I think what made Jack Coleman such a successful and popular president was his humanity. How many of us here today have sat in his office, or in the park or over a cup coffee, boring him with our problems?"

Sandy's voice, quiet to begin with, had become quieter as he read and, now, he seemed unable to continue. His hands were clenched on the edge of the podium, his head down so that his face was partially hidden from the audience. Suddenly his head came up. His face was red and he looked angry. He screwed his speech into a ball and threw it on the floor.

"I can't go on with this. Office gossip has made sure that everyone knows I didn't vote for this insane policy. It's crazy—the whole world's crazy! This won't solve our problems. People like Jack and Martha Coleman solve problems."

By now George Smart had reached the podium, as well as Joanne. Firmly, Joanne brushed off George's hand. She took Sandy's arm and led him from the podium and out of the room.

George bent the microphone back down to his size. "Sandy's emotion is shared by us all. We will all miss Jack and Martha Coleman. Jack's contribution to the Company today is another shining example of the humanity that Sandy spoke of. I would like you all to join with me in a toast of gratitude and farewell to Jack and Martha Coleman."

After the applause died down, Martha excused herself and went to the ladies' room. She mustn't stay long—it didn't help to have too much time to think and Jack needed her. Minutes later, with a fresh armor of powder and lipstick, she tucked in her stomach, held her head high and returned to the banquet hall.

The waiters had cleared a wide aisle between the tables and everyone was lining up along the aisle. Jack was looking around anxiously when she came in the door. He took a firm grip on her hand as she came up to him.

"Thought for a moment you'd chickened out on me!"

He smiled weakly.

An unnatural hush came over the room, rather shocking after the speeches and the frantic chatting. Martha was surprised. She thought the evening would really drag, but now she found herself longing for one more vacuous speech. But it was better this way. Although she and Jack hadn't been part of the detailed planning, they had heard some of the suggestions. George had wanted much more of a ceremony. Everyone remembered the waiters dressed as Cupids at his daughter's wedding. Somebody else had even wanted it all televised. No doubt such innovations would come in time. By then, it would probably be a compulsory rather than a voluntary policy. Thank goodness she and Jack wouldn't be around to see it.

Gripping each other's hands firmly, they both moved slowly down the aisle between the ranks of the silent, solemn audience. Some people smiled awkwardly, some reached out a tentative hand, but for the most part they looked embarrassed, as though they didn't really know how they should react. Martha and Jack smiled until their jaws ached. They moved through the ornate padded doors which swung shut behind them. For a brief moment, they were on their own in the small anteroom and they turned to each other in a quick embrace. Then the doors at the other side of the anteroom swung open and two young women in white uniforms came out and took them each by the arm.

On the other side of the anteroom, the rich red carpet and the embossed wallpaper gave way to highly polished vinyl floors and white high-gloss walls. The two women led them along a corridor and into a small changing room. "Would you like any help?" Jack declined for them and the women left. Martha slowly took off her dress. It was a nice dress; usually she had trouble finding things she liked. Too bad she wasn't going to get more use out of it. She folded it carefully and laid it in the box provided. She did this with every piece of clothing, smoothing all the wrinkles out of the pantyhose, placing the shoes exactly parallel.

"I never know whether these things go on with the opening at the front or the back," Martha indicated the new peach hospital gown. "I don't suppose it really matters this time," said Jack.

Martha tried to retrieve into her mind some of the folders of information on the New Retirement Policy. Pages of statistics flashed across her mind on the unemployment rate. The social, economic, psychological problems associated with unemployment, the high cost of government programs to assist the unemployed, the astronomical cost of care for the elderly, the rate of rural deterioration due to overpopulation, pollution due to overcrowding, the increase of malfunctioning organs among the under thirties; the graphs and charts came faster and faster. The door opened a couple of times but closed again. The third time a voice said, "Are we ready, then?"

The same two women escorted them down another corridor to a different room. In the middle of the room two high beds with brilliant white sheets were illuminated by a battery of glaring lights. One end of the room was screened off. Martha could hear subdued whispering and the surreptitious clinking of instruments coming from behind the screen.

The two women helped Jack and Martha up onto the narrow beds. They were still holding hands. Two masked and gowned figures came out from behind the screens. Martha tried to look into the eyes of the one nearest to her. The eyes behind the mask skittered away. There was complete silence, except for the rustle of preparation from behind the screen and the whir of some machinery in one corner. Martha barely felt the prick of the needle. As the waves of drowsiness washed over her, a memory collage of thoughts and pictures flooded into her mind. There was the doll with the ABC on its stomach, one leg coming off, and there was the faded yellow blanket that Grandma crocheted, one corner sucked and matted; there was Mother, packing Martha's clothes into a box; and Father digging out carrots to take to the Harvest Festival service. There were the daisies in the grass at Grandpa's place, and old Buster with his crooked tail, and Mike sucking his thumb, and a double scoop maple walnut cone, and waves breaking on the headland near Great- Aunt Ag's summer place, and Jack kissing her lightly that first time.

And there was nothing.

Dank and foul, dank and foul,
By the smoky town in its murky cowl;
Foul and dank, foul and dank,
By wharf and sewer and slimy bank;
Darker and darker the further I go,
Baser and baser the richer I grow;
Who dare sport with the sin-defiled?
Shrink from me, turn from me, mother and child.
                                    —Charles Kingsley

Boys Will Be Boys

At first, I was angry with Jimmy. I had looked forward to this trip for months, for years really. When he was just a little tyke, I fantasized about him growing up and me teaching him how to pitch a curve ball, how to tie a fly, but most of all, how to hunt. I had to admit that the anger went a whole lot deeper too. I wanted to be proud of Jimmy on this trip. I guess I wanted to show Bruce and Chuck that my son was a chip off the old block. I wanted Jimmy to get along with their boys, Steven and Chris, hell, I wanted him to be the leader of the pack. And now on the first morning of the trip, Jimmy takes off just when we're ready to go to the blind.

"He's a sensible kid. Probably just didn't want to come—get the impression he's not as keen on hunting as the rest of us—he'll come back as soon as we're gone," said Bruce as he poured coffee into the thermos.

"Too chicken to fire a gun," muttered Chris under his breath. His father Chuck glared at him before zipping up the tent. Nothing more was said, but I knew what they were thinking. The problem was, I agreed with them, and I hated that.

I had known Chuck and Bruce forever. Their fathers had been friends of my father and we all grew up in each other's pockets. As far back as I can remember, we'd competed with each other. How many sticks of gum can you cram in your mouth? How far can you spit watermelon seeds? How many RBI's did you get this year? How many girls have you kissed? The annual hunting trip had always been a big deal in our lives and a frenzy of competition. How much coffee can you drink and not have to pee in the night? How much coffee can you drink and how far can you walk around the campsite peeing all the way? How many shots fired to how many ducks downed—individually and by family?

The three of us went through school together and on to the local college. The competitiveness kept pace with our development. Who got the drunkest? Who got laid the most often? Who got married first? Who had the first kid, the first affair, the first divorce? The Hunting Trip had been part of our lives for as long as we could remember. The first time we went with our fathers, we were the same age as our boys are now.

Jimmy and Chris and Steven were all born within a few months of each other. I remember one drunken evening after one of them had been born—can't even remember which one—when we first planned *the Hunting Trip*, the first trip together with our boys after they turned twelve. Every year that we went, we talked about The Big Trip—when Jimmy was younger, he would always ask if this was the year that he got to come too.

It never crossed my mind that Jimmy might be anything other than crazy about such a trip—a chance to spend some quality time with his old man on his own, to camp in the wild and shoot some real live ducks. At first, I ignored his reluctance. I thought maybe he was sore about the divorce—I hadn't been spending as much time with him as I should and I knew Pat, his mom, was bitter about Rosie, my live-in.

"Maybe, he doesn't like killing something just for the fun of it," Pat snipped when I brought him back one evening.

"Come on Pat, I don't remember you ever turning down a tasty duck dinner, or some moose meat sausage, for that matter."

"Oh clever—get a dig in about my weight."

Jimmy began to slink upstairs as he always did when we argued. "Come on, son," I cajoled. "We'll have a grand time."

In the end, I blackmailed him—emotional blackmail, the worst kind. I really thought that he might not come and I just couldn't imagine going to Bruce and Chuck and telling them that Jimmy didn't want to come. Jimmy's always been a sensitive kid—too sensitive in my opinion. So I told him that Chuck and Bruce were my buddies and I wanted to show them what a fine boy I had and that I'd look really dumb if their boys came along and I had to make some excuse for him. I even told him he could bring his sketch pad—he wasn't a bad drawer for his age—drew funny stuff though—details of leaves and berries. When I was his age, I spent my time designing tanks.

I guess I kidded myself that it was all going to work out fine. Jimmy didn't join in much of the planning. It wasn't that he was a problem, he just didn't seem as enthusiastic as the other kids. I thought that once he got out there, he would miraculously become a fan. But, right from the start, it was sticky. We all piled into Chuck's Suburban for the ride up. Jimmy sat in the far back corner with his sketch pad, doodling away while Steven and Chris jostled and laughed beside him.

"You were a bit antisocial in the car there, Son," I said to him when we got out.

"They don't talk to me at school, Dad. Why should they want to talk to me now?"

"I thought you three were friends?"

"I've nothing against them, Dad—they're just different. They like different things."

"Like what?"

"They're into hockey and football and—and hunting and stuff."

"And you're not?" I began to feel dismayed.

"Well, I don't *not* like those things—I just like other stuff better."

At this point, I began to feel annoyed. "Well, why did you come on this trip then, if you don't like hunting?"

"You wanted me to, Dad."

To give Jimmy his due, he more than held his own on the hike into the campsite. It's a fairly long trek and, as usual, we had way too much stuff. Each year, we bring the same stuff and then some. This year, Chuck's new wife had made all sorts of goodies and he didn't have the heart to leave them behind. Our beer and bourbon capacity had gone up over the years, too. The other two boys complained about the weight of their packs right from the start, but Jimmy just marched along, his head bobbing from side to side as though he was photographing the brilliantly colored leaves and the rustling squirrels for future reference.

When we got to camp Bruce congratulated Jimmy on his carrying capacity. His son, Steven chipped in that Jimmy's pack was lighter than theirs.

"Oh, no it wasn't. If anything, it might even have been a bit heavier." I did the packing and I didn't want anyone to think that I was letting Jimmy off lightly. Jimmy smiled at me and I felt good.

Later that evening we sat around the campfire exchanging hunting stories, psyching ourselves up for the next day. Jimmy got quieter and quieter. The only time I saw him animated was when he trotted out the classic duck puzzler I had taught him.

MR DUCKS
MR NOT DUCKS
OSAR
WHALE OIL BEEF HOOKED
MR DUCKS

Chris and Steven were stumped. "Mr. Ducks? Mr. Ducks? Osar. Whale Oil Beef Hooked. Mr. Ducks? It doesn't make sense," Chris said while playing with his brand new skinning knife. He hadn't stopped sharpening it since dinner. Watching him play with it made me a bit uneasy. "Who cares about some dumb kid puzzle, anyway?" He hurled the knife at the tree across the campsite. It bounced off the tree narrowly missing his father's leg. "For Christ's sake, Chris, watch what you're doing. It's not a toy."

Chris retrieved the knife and sat sulking apart from the group. "Come on, Jimmy, you've got them stumped," I said. "Give them the answer."

Jimmy translated proudly:

'Em are ducks
'Em are not ducks
Oh yes, they are
Well, I'll be fooked!
'Em are ducks!

To give Bruce and Chuck their due, they didn't let on that it was an old joke. Steven was grudgingly impressed. Chris muttered under his breath. Jimmy glowed with pride. But the moment didn't last. Chuck and Bruce were knocking back the booze. I was embarrassed about some of the stories and jokes flying around. I thought Chuck shouldn't have laughed so loud when his son told the joke, "When is a squaw not a squaw ... when she's a mattress," or Chris' joke, "When a does a wolf cub become a boy scout? After he's eaten his first Brownie." And when they started asking about Rosie, I knew it was time to break out the sleeping bags. Rosie's my live-in, and she's, well, she's got great boobs, and I know I've told the lads a few stories. But that was in the bar, when it was just us. I guess they had more to drink than I did and didn't realize it was inappropriate. Chris, emboldened by his father's suggestions, even asked if she had brown or pink nipples. "Only squaws have brown nipples, you asshole," said Steven. At that, Jimmy bent his head even deeper over the sketch pad and scribbled furiously.

"I think it's time we hit the sack. Early start tomorrow," I said.

"Got you hot there, did we boy?" laughed Chuck. "No wanking in the sleeping bag, now." And they all, boys and fathers, all except Jimmy that is, laughed until they cried. Jimmy and I set about unrolling the bedrolls. I wanted to say something to him, but I didn't know what. I wanted to make it up to him.

"You all set for tomorrow?"

He nodded.

"Excited?"

"Guess so," he mumbled.

Chris came up to him, the knife that he had been sharpening still in his hand.

"Didn't see you sharpening your knife, Jimmy. We get to EVISCERATE the buggers. I can't wait."

"Oooh, big word there, Chris," said Jimmy, rather more quietly than I would have liked.

"Yeah, we have to do it right then and there while their guts are still steaming and their blood is still warm," added Steven. "Can't do it anywhere near the campsite. It attracts bears and wolves and stuff."

Jimmy turned pale and went into the tent he was sharing with Chris and Steve. They followed him in and I joined Chuck and Bruce in the bigger tent. I could hear Steve and Chris teasing Jimmy.

"You got your toothpaste in here, Jimmy? My dad says that the bears here are crazy about toothpaste."

"Going to dig the sucker's guts out with your bare hands, Jimmy? Your knife's so blunt you could pick your nose with it."

"Pick your ass, too!"

I lay there until the voices slowed and slurred to mumbles and were silent, but I could sense Jimmy's silent outrage across the campsite.

We woke later than we should have the next morning and Chuck and Bruce were not in the best of moods. Gone the days, I guess, when we could party all night and get up at the crack of dawn next day feeling like a million bucks. We had to call to the boys several times. I already had the fire going and the coffee pot on when Steven and Chris crawled out.

"Where's Jimmy?" I asked.

"Still cuddled up with his teddy bear," Chris sniped.

"He didn't bring that old..." I began.

"Just kidding, Mr. Brewster. I'll go wake him," laughed Chris.

"We'll both go," added Steven, and they both went back into the tent, malevolent grins on their faces. They were back a few seconds later. "He's not there, Mr. Brewster."

At first, I wasn't too worried. Jimmy had always been an early riser. Even when he was just a little tyke he would wake up early and lie on his back in his crib. One sunny summer morning I came in to find him smiling and gurgling, his little hands reaching out to the sunbeams dancing above his head. Later on, he would get up and play quietly with his bricks and Fisher-Price people. Now, when he slept over at my house, I would find him doodling in his sketchbook or on my new computer. He had probably gone off to do some drawing. When he didn't come back while we were eating breakfast or packing up, I began to get annoyed. He was doing this on purpose! He was sabotaging this trip that I'd been looking forward to for months, for years. The others obviously thought that too. I could hear Chris and Steven muttering under their breaths about wimps and babies. I knew that if I stayed behind to wait for him to come back, I would be furious—furious that my day's hunting had been spoiled, furious that he'd had made me look stupid in front of my friends. I wrote a note telling him tersely where we were going and we left.

It was a beautiful fall day. A weak sun sparkled on the glistening lichen. There was a slight touch of frost on the leaves rustling crisp underfoot, the warm smell of wood smoke in our hair. But I felt irritated. I trailed behind the others watching angrily as Bruce, one arm flung around his son's shoulders, broke into a bawdy song. Chuck and Chris ran up behind them silently and toppled them. The four of them rolled in the golden leaves heaving with laughter. I just strode on past and was the first to reach the lake.

We had been coming to the same little island every year for thirty years. "Our Island" we called it grandly, although it was barely big enough for us all, and it was so close to the shore you could wade out to it. That rusting tin chair had been my father's. I remembered the year I first strung the wire to dry our waders. I had been so proud of it. Dad walked into it later in the day. He said it was a dumb place to string a wire.

Chris and Steven had a grand time in the skiff positioning the decoys. There wouldn't have been room for Jimmy even if he had been there. And then we waited. We saw and heard ducks in the distance, but they weren't in the slightest bit interested in our duck calls—probably realized that no self-respecting ducks could keep it up for as long as Chris and Steven. The two of them got bored after the first ten minutes and began picking on each other now that Jimmy wasn't around. I couldn't concentrate on anything apart from Jimmy. One minute, I wished that he would appear and miraculously turn into an enthusiastic and talented marksman. The next, I fretted that he'd wandered off into the woods and was lost. The next, I had to restrain myself from storming back to camp and beating some spunk into him.

I just couldn't understand why he was like this. I remember the thrill of being taken along on my dad's hunting trips—that was the best. But suddenly, I touched the corner of a memory I had all but forgotten about. I saw myself out in a boat, on a choppy gray lake, on my own, streams of cold snot smeared on my tear-stained face. What was I doing out there? Then I remembered. I was sitting in the boat with my father, hidden in the reeds. My father blew repeatedly on his duck call. It was miserably cold and I was tired. I let out a huge yawn, and you know how you sometimes groan at the end of a yawn, well I did. And Dad went ballistic—as if the ducks could have heard it. He called his buddies, took off in **their** boat and left me, alone, for two hours. Why had I forgotten that? At least I wasn't like my old man? Or was I?

We were just about to cut our losses and move further down the lake when Skipper, Bruce's dog, growled softly. Steven and Chris stopped fidgeting. "Ducks?" Steven asked. "Right!" teased his Dad. "Ducks, crawling through the undergrowth—a rabbit, more like it, perhaps a coon or a fox. Target practice for you guys!" And he handed Chris his gun.

Before any of us had time to think, let alone to say anything, there was a slight movement behind us. Chris swung around and fired. Almost before I heard the report and small cry, I was on my feet, running.

Jimmy was lying, propped up against a tree, his sketch pad on his knee; at first, it looked as though he was sitting there, drawing. As I ran towards him, all I could see were his eyes. They were huge. I seemed to be moving so slowly. All sorts of thoughts, that must have taken longer than the twenty seconds or so that it took to reach him, flooded into my head.

His eyes were the weirdest color—a dark, flat, muddy brown, the color of the water in the old quarry up by Amundsen's place. I hadn't thought about it for years. It was a popular spot with kids in my day; an abandoned quarry filled with water. Nobody knew how deep the water was as you could never see through it, and nobody knew what was at the bottom. That was why it became a ritual, an initiation into the "in-crowd," to dive from the top of the ridge, some thirty-five feet up, into the brackish water.

I don't know why I went there that day in tenth grade. I think it was because Bruce and Chuck wanted to go, "just to see what was going on." They told me we would hide in the bushes and just watch. But the two of them made such a noise that it was obvious they wanted to be caught. A crowd of senior and junior guys were sitting around on the ridge—most of the football team and a few wannabes. They welcomed us with vicious smiles, dragging us over to sit on the edge of the ridge and relieve the oppressive boredom of a late summer afternoon.

Bruce and Chuck could hardly get their clothes off fast enough. Bruce did a perfect arcing dive into the muddy water and came up with a smile on his face and one fist raised in victory. Chuck was more reluctant, changed his mind about diving at the last minute and flopped into the water with a resounding smack. He took his time swimming to the edge, making sure his face was averted from the crowd, then sat with a fixed smile, biting his lip.

I've never been a strong swimmer. Oh yes, I could swim. But I never liked it, I never lost my fear of water. In fact, to this day, I'm still leery around water.

"Swimming's not my thing, guys," I said. "Swimming's not my thing," one of the wannabe's mimicked in my still high-pitched voice.

I stood up to leave, "I've got to get back, see you around..."

"Gotta get back to Mamma, boy?" sneered Sonny, the football quarterback, a guy whose IQ matched his collar size. He stuck out a foot as I sidled past and tripped me up. I didn't have time to pick myself up out of the dust before a couple of his goons grabbed me.

"Life's not as simple as that, kiddo," he continued. "You come up here and wanna play with the big boys, you gotta be tough like the big boys." Giggling maniacally, the two who had grabbed me, began pulling my clothes off. I fought as hard as I could. I remember them prying my fingers off the waistband of my shorts before wrenching them off. Then they dragged me over to the edge of the cliff and held me there, my hands pinned behind my back while the quarterback gave a little speech about his views on courage. I stared down at my puny white body, my smaller than average cock, and wished that I could die. I genuinely thought that I **was** going to die as they threw me over and I tumbled haphazardly into the water. I guess I screamed the whole way down and, when I surfaced, my mouth and lungs were full of foul-tasting water. Then I looked up and saw the ring of laughing faces against the sky, mouths wide in derision—with Chuck and Bruce laughing the loudest.

As soon as I reached Jimmy, I realized he wasn't dead. He had that same look of stunned bewilderment that a deer has when it lies in the woods, wounded but not finished. I found myself wondering if I would have the guts to put a bullet between his eyes to put him out of his misery or whether I would have to ask Chuck or Bruce to do it. I was still standing there when Chuck rushed past me to kneel by Jimmy's side.

"It's just a flesh wound," Chuck looked up at me.

I closed my eyes and braced myself for Chuck's final shot and was still standing there when I felt Bruce's hand on my arm.

"It's just a flesh wound—in his leg," Bruce said. "He's lost a bit of blood, but he'll be fine—we gotta get him out of here."

I opened my eyes then and stumbled over to where Jimmy lay. He stared up at me from a milky face; his teeth chattering violently despite the fact that he was biting his lip against the pain. He looked up at me, just as he used to when he dropped the ball when we played catch, "Sorry, Dad."

I stared down at him, the weirdest mix of emotions running through my mind. "Sorry, Jimmy? *You're* not the one who should be apologizing." And I bent and buried my face in his neck, smelling his fear, his vulnerability, and yes, his strength.

Chuck and Bruce flipped a coin to see who would come with me to carry Jimmy out to the car. Chuck won and a momentary flash of petulant anger crossed Bruce's face. His hunting trip was being ruined by stupid Jimmy Brewster, stupid Archie Brewster's son—like father, like son. Jimmy, despite his pain, kept apologizing to Chris, who had fired the gun, reassuring him that it wasn't his fault. "I should have known better."

We didn't talk much on the way out. Bruce set a fast pace with his end of the makeshift stretcher, sloughing off Jimmy's grunts of pain. "Faster we go, sooner you're out of here, kid." *And the sooner you're back to your hunting,* I thought.

Jimmy and I didn't talk much on the drive to the hospital either. In fact, we haven't talked about it much since then. There was so much I wanted to say, I just didn't know where to begin.

Instead, I found myself thinking about my father.

My father was always in control. The way he looked, for example. Brutally trimmed hair plastered to his head with hair cream, small military mustache, shirts starched to the point of discomfort. His days ran on a clockwork schedule and we all learned not to interfere. He left for the office at precisely 7:13 each morning. It seemed as though the house itself sighed when the front gate clicked shut behind him—Clara turned up her radio, Mama hummed as she cleaned up the kitchen, even Pogo thumped his tail on the worn linoleum beside the stove.

He was such a perfectionist; it was difficult to please him. It was my job to cut the grass in summer, shovel the driveway in winter, and no matter how hard I tried, I couldn't do it properly. His lawn always had pencil-straight mow lines, the corners by the driveway square and clean. He always managed to get right down to the cement with the snow shovel, even if someone had driven over the snow, although that was rare—Dad hated that.

That day as we carried Jimmy out, I vowed that I would never criticize him about his grass-cutting or snow shoveling, or, worse still, get out there and do it "properly" while he watched. And then I remembered that I lived in a condo.

I never saw my Dad cry, not even at Mama's funeral. Looking back on it, I guess the two of them didn't have such a great relationship. I knew she often took our side against him. I could hear her in the kitchen with her quiet voice, "They're just kids—don't be so hard on them." After she died, he withdrew into himself. He became more demanding, more obsessive. Our fridge was like a barracks bulletin board with rigid chore schedules and extra duty punishment rosters. The girls couldn't stand it. Clara got married right out of high school. Mary went off with her band.

I never saw him cry when he was well, I should say. But when he developed Alzheimer's, it seemed that was all he could do. The staff at the Home said he cried the most when we visited. Clara stopped coming. Mary and I went every week and then out for a beer. It was shortly before the end that we both admitted we liked him better the way he was now. "He probably wanted to be a sensitive, wear-your-heart-on-your-sleeve kind of guy all his life, but he got stuck in a control rut," Mary said.

I didn't really buy that at the time. But on that drive back into town, to the hospital with Jimmy, I began to wonder whether he did, in fact, have regrets about the kind of father he had been.

It wasn't like a lightning flash or anything, but I guess my life did begin to change slowly that day. I'm still divorced from Pat—too much hurt under that bridge. Rosie and I split up; she found someone who was "more fun" than me. I gradually stopped seeing Chuck and Bruce. Oh, we're still friendly if we bump into each other, but we don't go out of our way to meet. They still go hunting every year.

Jimmy's twenty-two now, a freelance cartoonist—doesn't make much money, but he really likes what he's doing. He's never had a girlfriend, lots of friends who are girls, but never a girlfriend. Yes, I wonder if he might be gay. Ten years ago, I would have freaked at the thought. Today all I feel is a kind of an undefined sadness. I know I'm still not ready to accept it, so I kind of ignore it, and Jimmy is so sensitive that I know he won't tell me until I'm ready. Every year, on the anniversary of *The Hunting Trip*, he phones me up and asks if I'd like to go hunting. We laugh a bit and then we go for a walk in the woods. I take my camera and Jimmy his sketchpad.

Plaid Dressing Gown

Green velour recliner
Shiny
Sagging
Pockmarked with cigarette burns
Sits
Empty.

Silence
Hangs in the room
Screams out for
Familiar creak of springs
Walrus breathing
Over the hum of TV
Click of dentures
Digestive protestations of
The evening's beef link sausages and beans.

Plaid dressing gown
Hangs
Empty on the back of the door
Smelling of
Humbugs
Tobacco
Old teddy bears.

Open drawer by the bed
Small leather bound prayer book
Pages loose
Fragrant with use
Swan Vestas wooden matches
Curiously Strong Mints
Tensor bandages

Crumbling childhood drawings - mine?
Curled-edge, sepia photo of girl in 1930 two-piece bathing suit
Familiar? Familial?

I lie in my old room
Still
The middle window rattles when the bus goes by
Third board from the door squeaks
Doves on the lawn whisper myths of childhood dawn.

Where is the creak of my father's door?
The blare of early morning radio?
Uneven steps past my door, chamber pot in hand?
Hacking morning cough?
Laboured breathing on the stairs?
Kettle singing below?
Saturday smell of burnt sausage?

I can hear
I can see
I can smell
But I cannot touch
My memories.

Lewis Carroll Defines a Father's Death

'Twas brillig, and the slithy toves
Did gyre and gimble in the wabe:
All mimsy were the borogoves,
And the mome raths outgrabe

The irony is it **is** brillig
Fat pigeons and scruffy squirrels gyre and gimble in the wabe
While I sit
In my father's empty room
Mimsy
Beyond mimsy

Beware the Jabberwock, my son!
The jaws that bite, the claws that catch!
Beware the Jubjub bird, and shun
The frumious Bandersnatch!

He fought them all
My father
The gaily plumed Jubjub bird
Beckoning from the bottom of the bottle
The frumious Bandersnatch
Coaxial cable claws tipped with gall
Digging in to the psyche
And now the Jabbberwock
The jaws that bite, the claws that catch
Us all.

Where was I
When the Jabberwock, with eyes of flame
Came whiffling through the tulgey wood?

Why did I live five thousand miles from the Tumtum tree,
My vorpal blade useless in its sheath,
And only came galumphing back
After the Jabberwock had slain my father?

But suddenly he is here
At the old kitchen table
The one we used to have
Still laden with memories of poetic feasts
He sits
Fork in hand
Crumb on tie
Fleck of spittle in the corner of his mouth
O frabjous day! Callooh! Callay!
He chortles in his joy.

Christmas Junkie

Mom's real funny about Christmas. She's not the mushy sort, usually, but she really goes overboard about Christmas. It starts in October, probably before, but it gets to be a pain in the butt then. The first thing is the baking—the Plum Pudding. Jesse and me have to stir—don't ask *me* why—some dumb old tradition I guess. This year was so embarrassing; Melanie was over and we were trying out her new eye-shadow and Mom had the nerve to call me down for the stirring ceremony. Her Christmas cake is always dry and brick hard—despite the fact that she pours half a bottle of Dad's brandy over it. She usually ends up giving it to the mailman—I bet he dumps it in the Wilkinson's garbage next door. And we don't need all that other stuff—some of it is okay. I like the chocolate fudge and the lemon curd tarts, but she makes way too much and ends up eating most of it herself and then spending the next few months on one of her dumb diets.

And then there's the shopping. If she's not shopping she's down in the basement pouring over endless lists written on the backs of envelopes. It's such a waste of time—Dad always takes his stuff back and changes it. He hates shopping. One year he put a check in a big box and wrapped it up—Jeez, did that one backfire!

The closer the big day comes, the crazier the activity. Mom's always going on about how she hates the commercialization of Christmas and how people shouldn't do anything about Christmas until the middle of December. Ha! She *does* stand firm about when we get the tree though—no earlier than the weekend before. But we can't just go down to the local tree lot—oh no! We have to go out and cut one down—and we *all* have to go. "It's part of our family tradition." It wastes a whole day. We have to drive for hours, and then walk for miles as all the good trees near the road are taken by that time. It's always a shit-awful day—freezing fog or snowing—not the big, fat flakes you see floating down on Christmas cards, but the kind that come at you sideways on the wind—and everyone's always in a lousy mood. And we have yet to find the perfect tree. Mom bounces ahead looking for *The Tree.* In the end, we pick some little runt that's crooked or bald on one side, just so we can get the hell home.

And we're *still* not off the hook. We have to get the thing into the house. That's always quite the production. You know, I sometimes wonder how Dad holds down a job as an engineer. He can't even get a Christmas tree to stand up straight. I don't remember a single year when the frigging thing didn't fall over, *after* it's been decorated of course. When it's finally standing, Dad's usually in a foul mood, so *he* gets to slump in front of the tube with a beer. We're still on duty. Out comes the box of decorations. They're a real mish-mash of things—most of them pretty tacky. But Mom wouldn't part with a single one. The angel at the top is the one she had as a child—fallen angel, more like—her hair is falling out, she's lost an eye, her wings are drooping and her dress is as gray as city snow in March. Each decoration means something—the first Christmas they were married, the year we were born, some really dumb stuff me and Jesse made in play school. And then there's the candy. Mom makes these little chocolate Santas and bells that *her* Mom used to make back in England. They take *forever* and end up looking like little dog turds. We have to wrap each one and tie red wool on—that takes forever too. When we were little, we were allowed to eat one a day. Then Jesse and his friends took to eating them all the first day the tree was up. Now, Mom eats them all as she takes the tree down after Christmas.

Decorating the tree takes forever. Mom wants it to be just perfect. When it's done, we take off and Mom turns all the lights out, apart from the Christmas lights, and listens to the same old tape every year—a bunch of little boys singing churchy music.

Talking about church, that's the other really dumb thing about the season. We don't set foot inside a church from one Christmas to the next. Oh, we used to go when were little. When I was about six, Mom suddenly got all gung-ho about God and dragged us off to church—she even taught Sunday School for a couple of years. Dad never came. Then, Jesse started having hockey on Sundays and Mom had some kind of run-in with the old Holy Mary who ran the Sunday School, and we just stopped going. But come Christmas, back we all go. I think it's pretty hypocritical, but even Dad goes along with it. "Just humor your mother. It's important to her." At least we don't have to go on Christmas morning anymore. No, we have to go on Christmas Eve. At first we always went to the Family Service along with all the yowling kids who had never been inside a church in their lives. And then, a couple of years ago, we graduated to the midnight service. I don't mind it that much—it's kind of cool—lots of candles everywhere—heavy on the music, light on the mumbo jumbo which suits me just fine.

I kind of like the actual day, or at least part of it. Mom is the greatest Santa. She finds the neatest things to put in our stockings. No wonder she spends so much time shopping. I never see things like that in the stores. This year there were socks with Scotty dogs all over them, I have a thing about Scotty dogs, those little Japanese seeds that grow into these awesome flowers, my own personalized mailing labels complete with a Scotty dog logo.

Mom's always up before us, waiting for us to wake up and open our stockings. *She* always has a pretty tacky stocking. Dad says he doesn't have the time. I don't think she minds—she's too busy watching us and Dad. His stocking is always the same—a Giles cartoon book, a bar of Toblerone chocolate, a tin of peppermint humbugs and some skimpy underpants—gross!

We open our stockings in our pajamas and then we all have to go and get dressed before breakfast. When we were little, Mom had to take photos to send back to Gran and Gramps and she told us they would much rather see us in clothes. But Gramps is long gone and Gran couldn't fit any more photos into her little room at the Sunnyside Eventide Home—what a dumb name—so I don't see what the point of it is. Old habits die hard, I guess.

Of course, everyone likes opening presents. Some of the kids at school always seem to be disappointed with their Christmas presents, but not me. Mom does go a bit overboard at Christmas. Dad's always bugging her about it, but since she got some money after Gramps died he's quit bitching about it. Like, she doesn't spoil us—like some kids who say they want a Northface Jacket and their Mom just goes out and buys it. She's funny about other things—like GI Joes. All Jesse wanted for years was GI Joe stuff, but Mom never gave in. And she won't let me get one of those bathing suits with the real high-cut legs.

It's after the present opening that the day starts to go sour. Other kids complain that their Christmas Day is so busy and noisy. They have grandparents for breakfast, go for lunch to Cousin Arty and then have twenty-three for dinner which starts at three in the afternoon. We don't have any grandparents, aunts, uncles, cousins, or whatever, in town. In fact, our nearest relatives are five thousand miles away, in jolly old England.

It would be OK if we could treat it like any other day—watch the tube, play some video games, or visit some friends. But the friends are all tied up with their families. Even the frigging Mall is closed. Mom thinks we should do something "as a family" so we usually end up going for a walk or skating, "to work up an appetite for dinner." Both Jesse and me are allergic to walks so we kind of lag behind while Mom and Dad stride ahead arm in arm wearing their "aren't we the happy family on Christmas Day" expressions. At least it doesn't last too long, as Mom has to get back to get the turkey in the oven. And after we've watched the Queen squinting at the teleprompter and the royal grandchildren chasing the royal corgis, we're off the hook for an hour or two.

And then comes the high point of the day as far as Mom

is concerned—the Christmas dinner. Once we had it on our own—just the four of us—I think someone was sick—yeah, Jesse had the chickenpox—and that year it was cool. But usually we have to get together with other people. We always have the Mendelmanns. Mrs. M. went to school with Mom way back in England. She married this Jewish fellow and converted. They have these two nerdy little boys who bring the sickest selection of jokes and tricks and do things like let the hamster out or draw a moustache on your new Smashing Pumpkins poster. Mrs. M. is obviously like Mom—a Christmas junkie. But worse, as she can't have it anymore. Mr. Mendelmann is real strict. Once Mom forgot and put bacon in the stuffing and he picked every last little piece out and left it on the side of the plate. They didn't come for a couple of years after that. Mom invites other people, too. At least she's stopped asking strangers, ever since that homeless guy she met at the bus shelter walked off with three silver spoons. But she always includes some other lame duck.

After everyone goes home, Dad shuffles off to bed muttering about how he'll do the dishes in the morning. Mum clears away the worst of the mess and then puts another churchy tape on and sits in front of the fire with an eggnog. That's another thing I like about Christmas—last year I snuck one with booze in it—yuck! This year I sat with her—she had grated real chocolate and cinnamon to sprinkle on top of the eggnog. The tape finished and it was kind of nice, being so quiet. I could hear the fire sputtering, could hear Flossie's stomach grumbling from too many doggie leftovers, I could hear Jesse playing his new CD up in his room, and—I could hear Mom snoring! I looked over at her and she was asleep with this big smile on her face, a purple paper hat falling over one eye. I straightened her crown and gave her a kiss—hell, she was asleep, and went up to bed and my new red flannel nightie with the Scotty dog Mom had sewn on the front.

A Birthday Gift

83 years old today
83 bloody years, for God's sake
For **God's** sake?
Fat lot of good He's ever done in my life
He took my man and left me
Moldering on
Arthritic bones bitching night and day
"It's time to go, time to go..."
Skin dry and wrinkled
A creeping blight of liverspots and eczema.
Bloody God took my beautiful son
So many empty years ago.

Left me a daughter, my second child
And **she** lives in Canada
Cold, inhospitable, **distant** Canada
No birthday visits from the grandchildren
No little holidays to the cottage on the Channel Islands
For **this** octogenarian
Just the old stiff upper lip on the phone
As **she** gets upset if I moan
Feels guilty I shouldn't wonder.

Now who could that be ringing the door bell
At four o'clock in the afternoon
Penance roses from Canada?
Belgian truffles from some swag-shouldered suitor?

"You Mrs. McPhee?
Where do ye want these three bags o' manure ye ordered?
Ye did order manure, didn't ye?

Mud in the eye!
Manure in the eye!
God lives
Justice lives
Divine excrement
Three bags of shit
For the old bag of shit
On her 83rd birthday!

Pieta

Burning pain
Out of centuries cold marble
Through the babel of a gaggle of French teenagers
Across the chasm of a sixties ego.

I stand
Pasta/bread/chianti/grass dozy
In the commercial chaos
That is St. Peter's Basilica in July
Accidentally/on purpose
Stepping on Gallic toes
For a better view of the Pieta
Can't get too close
Sturdy barrier, burly security
Guard Jesus' toes against souvenir hungry tourists.

The flashfire of agony
Sends me reeling
Stepping on more toes
"Sorry...scusi..."

Naked grief
Mary's life and Jesus' broken body
Growing cold and stiff
Eyes, shoulders, trailing fingers
Speak a mother's daily dread
No surprise, little anger
Only the realization
That her worst fear
Is here.

And I cry for Him
For Jesus
For my dead brother
Ordinary miracle to family and friends
For Mary
For my mother
Who could not save him with her anxious love
Who cannot let him go.

For myself
Whose mere survival
Casts me as Judas.

Ronka's Tale

Ronka saw the boy on one of her first trips to Park Point. It was a fine, early-fall day. The leaves were just beginning to change color, their fiery rusts and golds made the lake seem even bluer.

The lake was the *only* good thing about Duluth. Moving here had been, without a doubt, the worst thing that ever happened to Ronka in all fifteen years of her life. Earlier in the summer she had been dragged out of a perfectly good life, a perfectly *wonderful* life in a big, exciting Canadian city to small town, middle U.S.A.—Duluth, Dull-fucking-uth—population 85,000. Economy: struggling. Climate: the pits. And why? Because her father had been transferred—A "great career move," he called it.

As she lay on the sand, she realized she wasn't mad at her father. She didn't know how she felt—even **if** she felt. She was half asleep, her eyelids bobbing with the gentle swell of the waves, when she first noticed someone swimming. She sat up, the first tinglings of an electric energy flowing through her.

It was good to feel that energy, feel anything, after all these weeks. The first few days had been hell. Since then, she had gone into emotional hibernation. The rest of the family decided to put a brave face on it. Robbie, the little rat, seduced by tales of American 24-hour cartoon networks, MTV, junior high football and the like, was even quite enthusiastic. Mom, who'd bitched like crazy to begin with, had done an about-face and, between keeping half the decorators in town busy, was compiling her personal list of *The Seven Wonders of Duluth*.

Although she kept it to herself, Ronka agreed when it came to the Lake. She'd never been into scenery before—in fact she had ruined many a good holiday fighting with Robbie in the back seat of the car while their parents "oohed" and "aahed" over snow-capped peaks or waves breaking against headlands. But this lake was different. It was so—so enormous. You just couldn't get away from it. No matter where you went, it was always there. You'd round a corner and suddenly you were blinded by this huge expanse of water—shining blue—or gray—even black. That was another neat thing about it—it changed, had wild mood swings, just like she did. One day it was glassy smooth, gentle ripples teasing the rolling pebbles at the water's edge. The next, it was an angry gray-pink, the wind whipping the tops off the waves, sand-laden water forcing its way up the beach, into your ears, your hair, your mouth, your lungs.

Swimming is not something people do in Lake Superior. It's not just that it's too cold; it's almost as though there's an invisible sign, <u>Gods Only! Mortals Swim at your own Risk!</u> Ronka had dared to swim in the Lake during those first few days. It was so hot, a freak heat spell, everyone said. Ronka kept going back in, to get away from the burning sand. Each time she swam further and further out. She floated on her back, her long hair streaming behind her, her ears underwater so she could hear only the thrum of the Lake and see only the blue sky. If she was careful not to let her legs drop down to the deeper, colder water, she could lie suspended like that for a few minutes before getting too cold. But all the time, she felt as though she was trespassing, that a scaly tentacle might reach up from the depths and claim her. And she certainly wouldn't consider swimming today; it was warm but it **was** early fall. Yet there, not a hundred yards away, breaking the cool blue plain, something, someone was swimming. At first she thought it might be a bird or some kind of fish—perhaps even a mythical lake monster. She squinted against the sun and tried to make out who or what it was.

Ronka remembered the first time she and her mom walked at Park Point with Rusty, the family dog, who wildly shared Ronka's enthusiasm for the beach. They walked past all the houses along the sloping sand. Her mom kept wanting to turn back but Ronka urged her on. It was another beautiful day—the Lake was mirror smooth and the sun felt good on Ronka's bare legs. When they finally did turn around, they were in a different world. The sky behind them had secretly turned black; angry storm clouds jostled for position along the skyline; a feisty north wind whipped the waves into frothy egg white. By the time they reached the car, the swirling sand was stinging their legs, the rain had started in earnest and they were soaked. On the way home the rain stopped and the sun came out again and shone off the tossing waves and the rusting hull of an ore boat carving a route toward the Lift Bridge and the inner harbor.

As the swimmer got closer, she saw it was a girl—no, a boy, with chin-length hair, the kind of hair that was blond even when wet. He swam into the shallows right in front of her and stood in the waist deep water. A silver current ran from his honey-colored skin. Ronka drew a deep breath. Now **this** was one up on the offerings at the Marshall School.

Her parents had decided to put her into Duluth's only private school—terrified, no doubt, by Canadian newspaper reports of gun-toting, heroin-mainlining, orally-sexually active (now that **was** gross) teenagers roaming the hallways of all American high schools. The kids at the private school were nice—N.I.C.E. They spoke to her, and included her in their outings to Perkins. One girl even made her a cute little card welcoming her to Duluth. That almost made it worse. She felt so different from them and she wasn't sure that she wanted to change just to fit in.

The boy flicked his wet hair out of his green/blue eyes and smiled the kind of smile that made the sun seem brighter. "Coming for a swim?" he asked. Ronka was almost speechless, "I—I didn't bring my suit—isn't it too cold—where did you come from?"

The boy didn't wait for her to finish, but with another smile and a wave, he sank back into the water. He cavorted in the lake in front of her, one minute swimming languorously up and down, the next diving, swimming for what seemed endless minutes underwater until, with a flash of golden skin, he surfaced with a shout of joy. Ronka wondered if he was swimming naked.

Then, suddenly, he was gone. She looked away for a moment at a passing bird and when she looked back at the lake, he was gone. At first she was anxious. She paced up and down the shore searching for some sign of him. But he didn't reappear. So, reluctantly, she called Rusty and they began the long walk home.

She couldn't keep away from the lake after that. At first, her mother was pleased that she was enthusiastic about something in their new hometown. And, to begin with, Ronka would gladly accompany her mother on any trips to the Lake. Up the North Shore, it was completely different—wilder, even less predictable. At the mouth of the Lester River, old fishermen perched on shining rocks. Their wind and time-blasted faces looked out across the water. An old tackle box and a battered thermos lay on the rocks at their feet, birds circling above them impatient for some action. Further up the shore on a blustery day's drive, the benign blue turned grump gray, waves smacked against inaccessible headlands, the ghostly groaning of foundered ships echoed in every gust of wind.

But for Ronka, the Lake only existed on Park Point. She went there almost every day after school. Sometimes the boy was there and sometimes he wasn't. Sometimes he talked to her and sometimes he didn't. He didn't ask her to swim with him again until a couple of weeks later. A brisk September wind was blowing. Normal people would not have considered getting wet. But Ronka didn't even think twice. It was weird—she actually felt comfortable, as if she could stay in forever.

They swam every day after that, at first just up and down the shore. She stopped taking Rusty along. He made such a fuss when she went swimming, racing up and down barking furiously and finally going back to her towel where he sat whining until she came out. Several times she asked the boy to come and sit with her on the sand and share her sandwich. He always refused, saying that he was more at home in the water. He never told her his name, or talked about where he came from or where he went to. He just laughed and swam off.

It wasn't long before Ronka realized that her mother knew

she was lying about going over to friends' houses. Finally Ronka admitted she was at the Lake every day. She could tell that her mother either didn't believe it or thought she was really strange. Her mom kept on about it, "I know you miss your old friends, dear. But you've got to make an effort. Why don't you try out for the school play? Or the basketball team? What do you do at the Lake all by yourself? I don't know how safe it is down there."

Ronka would just smile and say as she left, "Don't worry, Mom. I'm not unhappy here. I like the kids at school. I just really like sitting by the Lake; it makes me feel happy." Ronka's dad, who was always away on business trips, made little of the mother's concerns—"Kid seems happy to me, she's a teenager, for Christ's sake. Just a stage. Let her be."

So Ronka spent more and more time at the Lake.

Sometimes, she even slipped out at night. She never told the boy when she was coming, but he was always there. One night in early October the sky was studded with stars and a full moon shone a long path across the lake. She saw the boy swimming towards the shore, his hair silver in the moonlight. He suggested that they swim over to some caves down the coastline. Ronka protested. "That's like—like miles. I can't swim that far—let alone that far and get back home before breakfast."

"I can," laughed the boy. "Hold around my neck."

It was sheer heaven. With her hands clasped around his neck, her face pressed into his lake-sweet hair, they raced through the water. Cocooned in soft darkness, body and soul sucked into the fantasy, she was totally absorbed, consumed. When he finally slowed down, she was reluctant to let go. Her body rested against his, her heart fluttering into his smooth back, her legs floating down to rest on his legs—

Suddenly she knew why he never came out of the water—he had no legs—instead a fish tail—a shimmering fish tail, that could be hard with energy as it drove them through the water, or flip gently back and forth as they rested in the shallows. They sat together on a rock. The moonlight shimmered silver and green and blue on his wonderful tail. Ronka couldn't take her eyes off him, he was so beautiful. She reached down into the water and splashed handfuls of phosphorescent water onto his tail, tracing the drops with her fingers as they ran down through the shining scales.

Ronka started to skip school. When she did attend, she didn't work, she just sat in class daydreaming and doodling and smiling to herself. The school counselor called her mom and they had a big conference. Ronka sat in the counselor's office smiling and didn't answer any of their questions. *What are you so unhappy about? Why do you feel the need to go to the Lake? What do you do there? Do you meet other kids down there? Have they been giving you anything? Alcohol? Drugs? Are they making you do things you don't want to do? Why are you doing this to us?*

The following week her parents took her to a psychiatrist at the Duluth Clinic. At least he didn't try and make her talk, instead he gave her crayons and told her to draw and doodle while he talked. She went back to see him every day for two weeks and then he called her parents in. Ronka didn't really listen to what they were saying. The psychiatrist had a fancy office overlooking the Lake. It was so foggy outside that she could hardly tell where the fog ended and the Lake began, but she knew it was there—*he* was there. The psychiatrist used lots of long words and technical terms to tell Ronka's anxious parents that they had nothing to worry about; that Ronka was a fine young woman going through a difficult transition in her life and that she had chosen the Lake as her "friend" to help her through that transition. The best thing they could do was to relax and be loving and caring and, before they knew it, she would be out of this stage and back to being a normal, noisy teenager driving them all crazy. He laughed at his own joke.

Ronka's dad sat silently, nodding as though it all made sense and he'd known it all along. But her Mom was more skeptical. "You mean we just let her wander off to the Lake whenever she wants? How do you know there's not some gang down there that she's connecting with? And she swims, you know, Doctor. She swims—in Lake Superior—in October! And what about her safety—she's all on he own—she could be attacked, abducted, raped!" At this, the doctor smiled and patted Ronka's mom on the shoulder. "This is Duluth, Mrs. Simpson. Don't worry. Just leave her be. In a matter of weeks, this will all seem like a bad dream."

And so they went home. Ronka's dad went off on another business trip and her mother fretted silently. Ronka got up in the mornings and had breakfast and left the house. Sometimes she went to school, sometimes she went to the Lake. The days got shorter, the leaves turned red, golden, brown and then swirled off the trees. Some mornings the water's edge was white with frost or ice. But the boy was still here, still swimming and playing in the waves. And every day Ronka would swim with him, every day a little bit further and a little bit deeper and every day she felt she would never be any happier.

But then she was.

One morning, Ronka did not come back. Her mother slept in because she had finished a bottle of scotch on her own the night before. She prayed to a God she hadn't prayed to in years that Ronka had risen early and gone to school. When she found that Ronka wasn't at school, she prayed that she had gone down to the Lake and would be back by three—or five or sometime. That evening. she called Ronka's dad at his hotel. He took the next flight back and initiated a flurry of investigation. They found Ronka's clothes in a small tidy heap under a piece of driftwood—but nothing else.

———

A year later, Ronka's dad is away on another business trip. Robbie is at boarding school in Ontario. Mom, wearing one of Ronka's old jackets, a fifth of vodka in one pocket, sits all day on a piece of driftwood on Park Point, scanning the vast water.

Home Hunting

Jeffrey could smell the burnt toast through the wide open front door as he walked up the narrow path. He peered anxiously through the smoke as he went into the small bungalow. "Ma? Are you alright?"

There was no answer. Not surprising, as the radio was blaring a Souza march and his mother was half deaf. He stepped over the cat's litter box, wrinkling his nose. His shiny brown brogues crunched on the spilled litter. He found his mother in the bathroom. She was singing along with Souza and squinting into the toothpaste-flecked mirror.

Isabel Keene turned as she saw her son, offering a heavily rouged cheek for a kiss. "Give me a hand with these, there's a dear—can't see worth a damn without my glasses and can't apply these damn things with them on!" She wheezed with laughter which turned into a deep, sloughing cough. She thrust a set of false eyelashes into her son's hand.

"You don't need these, Ma. You don't need to dress up. We're just..."

"Oh, but I do. Got to show that I'm not the old fart they expect."

"But you look fine as you are and, anyway, you need glue for these things."

"I do? It must be in here somewhere."

As she rooted in the bathroom cabinet, Jeffrey scanned his mother. She had dressed for the occasion. A little Jackie Kennedy pillbox with veil, fur tippet complete with head and glass eyes draped over a lime green blouse with frilled collar, black mohair skirt amply flecked with cat hair, black stockings with seams and runs, cork heeled shoes.

"Always wondered where those spare teeth went to," she said, flinging the falsies on the floor. "Never knew I had so many tubes of Preparation H, just as well."

She picked up a white plastic pouch. "Here's a rave from the grave. Don't need this anymore. And then again, maybe some of these old geezers have some life left in them." And instead of throwing the vaginal douche on the floor with the rest of the stuff, she put it back in the cupboard.

"Ma, we have to go. Our first appointment is for ten. You look fine without the eyelashes, honest."

She turned to him and pinched his cheek. "You always were a flatterer. Can't understand why you never married."

On the way out, Jeffrey checked the kitchen. The oven was still on, set to broil, and the remains of the charred toast were a soggy mess in the sink. "Why don't you use the toaster I gave you, Ma?"

"Bloody useless!" she snorted. "Toast's always limp and flaccid. I like it hard and brown." Her old eyes twinkled with mischief.

"Mother," Jeffrey protested. "Can you please tone it down for today. We want to make a good impression, don't we?"

"Not particularly," his mother answered. "S'not as though I'm going into one of those places."

"Mother," Jeffrey wheedled. "You said you'd keep an open mind..."

"Oh, alright...let's go rattle a few wheelchairs, then."

Jeffrey had been busy in the few days he had been "home" in Henley. He still referred to Henley as "home" although he had now lived in Baltimore for 18 years. He took a week's vacation to come over and "sort his mother out." He must have checked out a dozen homes in the past three days and had chosen three for his mother to look at. He decided to keep the best for last, or rather he purposely chose to visit Shady Acres first. He would never dream of putting his mother into such a place, but he knew it would highlight the benefits of the other two homes on his list.

Shady Acres looked impressive at first sight. Imposing stone gates, a winding driveway through an archway of trees, a solid Victorian house. It all looked respectable.

"Far too grand for me," Jeffrey's mother snorted as they came down the driveway. "Kind of place where everyone's name is hyphenated and they keep a copy of Burke's Peerage on the bedside table."

Jeffrey didn't say anything. He parked the car and went to help his mother. She swung her legs out, gave him her hand and tried to push herself up with her other hand on the door jamb.

"Come on Jeffrey, pull! You're getting awfully puny. I thought you'd bought into the American fitness crap—what's that video they advertise on TV here—*Buns of Steel*. Load of bollocks if you ask me."

"Sorry, Mother, I didn't realize how much help you needed." And he yanked rather forcefully on her arm, popping her out of the car like a cork out of a bottle. He looked at his mother apologetically, but she just laughed. "Ooh, I do **love** a strong man!"

Her laugh faded as she looked around. Close up, Shady Acres was bleak. Murky stone, peeling, steel-gray paint work, old slate roof in a sad state of repair, dark, overgrown bushes and ivy. She shivered.

"Cheerful little pile, eh? Wonder where they buried the body?"

Jeffrey took his mother's arm and they went in. The entrance lobby was cavernous—dark, cold and silent. Isabel wrinkled her nose. "What's that foul smell. God, that takes me back. Boarding school. Boiled cabbage."

Yes, that was it, Jeffrey thought. *That was why this place gave him the shivers. Branscombe Hall Preparatory School for Boys.*

"We should never have sent you to that place. You were far too young. Your father's idea. Never bought his 'bit of buggery never did **me** any harm' nonsense."

Now it was Jeffrey's turn to shiver. "Come on, Ma, let's go. This is just the first place—and to be quite honest, it's not..."

One of the many closed doors opened and a small man backed out, talking to someone inside the room.

"I don't care how much Cook complains. She'll just have to bulk it up with beans or rice or wallpaper paste for all I care."

The man turned, his little moustache twitching with irritation. His scowl changed to an obsequious smile as he saw Jeffrey and his mother.

"Oh, Mr. Keene. You startled me. And this must be your dear mother."

He advanced on Jeffrey's mother, both hands extended.

"Yes, this is my mother, Isabel Keene," Jeffrey said. "Mother, this is Mr. Pilkington-Smith, the director of Shady Acres."

Isabel Keene lowered her bifocals to inspect the little man from head to toe. "Heil Pilkington-Smith," she muttered under her breath.

"I beg your pardon?"

Jeffrey glared at his mother. "Let's look around, shall we, before my mother gets, er, tired."

Mr. Pilkington-Smith explained that Shady Acres had been a private home until recently. "And the owners, an elderly couple themselves, rather let the place slip. We're embarking on a ten-year renovation project."

"Most of us won't be around in ten years," interrupted Jeffrey's mother.

Conditions deteriorated as they left the hall and office. Mr. Pilkington-Smith led them into a large room that must have been impressive in its day. Filled with fusty furniture on a threadbare carpet, it was now dark and cold and empty.

"Why is it so cold?" asked Mrs. Keene.

"Well, we don't use this room on a daily basis. We gather here for our musical soirées—very popular with our residents."

"But it's not just here—whole place—except for your stuffy little office—is as cold as an undertaker's waiting room." Mr. Pilkington-Smith looked down at his shiny, tiny black shoes. "As we age," he announced pompously, "our internal thermostats fluctuate. We've noticed that our residents are more comfortable when it's cooler..."

Isabel followed his look down to his shoes. "Gollygosh, what **shiny** little shoes! But that's bullshit, if you'll pardon my French. I'm old and I can assure you I'm even more cantankerous when I'm cold."

"Well, most of our residents prefer to sit in the conservatory during the day." He opened another door with a flourish and ushered them in. Isabel took a couple of steps and then stopped suddenly.

"Oh dear! Exceeds my wildest dreams," she murmured.

The room was brighter and marginally warmer than the rest of the house. It was full of people, yet there was an uncanny silence. About half the occupants of the room were in wheel chairs. Slouched figures were grouped around tables, but there was no communication between them. Two surly nurses stood by the window, one with arms folded across her none-too-clean apron, the other guiltily stubbing out a cigarette. The smell of boiling cabbage was overwhelmed by another even less pleasant smell—urine."

Mrs. Keene wrinkled her nose again. "Samuel. That's it—Samuel."

Jeffrey smiled behind his hand. Samuel the spaniel **had** smelt like that just before he died.

"What do they **do** here all day?" his mother asked querulously.

"Well, they're not here all day—just in the morning until lunch-time," defended Mr. Pilkington-Smith.

"What do you do here?" Isabel asked a wispy-haired

woman sitting close by.

The woman turned slowly, dreamily and gazed at Isabel with pale, watery eyes. "Nothing," she whispered. "Nothing." She reached out a shaking hand to Isabel. "Will **you** take me home. Alan and Ruth have ganged up against me—but **you** can take me home—**please,** I want to go home."

"Don't be silly Dottie—Alan and Ruth want the best for you—that's why you're here," said Mr. Pilkington-Smith as he firmly took hold of the woman's arms, pulling one sleeve down over a large bruise and beckoning to the nurse who came over and wheeled her away.

"Mrs. Hutchinson is one of our frailer...always falling..." Pilkington-Smith spoke loudly to drown out Mrs. Hutchinson's wailing.

Isabel suddenly turned to Jeffrey and grasped his arm. "I've seen enough, Jeffrey. Let's go."

She dragged him out of the room and sped through the cold corridors. They were followed by a hand-wringing Pilkington-Smith. "But we haven't seen the rooms—let me give you our brochure."

Jeffrey called back over his shoulder. "Thanks for your time, Mr. Pilkington-Smith. I'll be in touch."

In the car Jeffrey's mother sat silently, her mouth pursed into an angry-hurt line. Jeffrey shot her anxious little glances as they drove down the driveway.

"Keep your eyes on the road Jeffrey! Unless you plan to crash me into a tree and solve all your problems that way."

"Mother!"

Mrs. Keene snorted and crossed her arms over the purse on her lap.

Jeffrey continued his furtive glances, until his mother sighed, uncrossed her arms and turned to pat him on the knee.

"Don't look so anxious, Jeffrey. I know that you

wouldn't stuff me into a place like that. I may follow through when I fart, but there's nothing wrong with my mind. That was the horror home which will make the others look **so** appealing in comparison—right?"

Jeffrey started with surprise, then looked sheepish and laughed.

"You're right, Ma...I never could fool you, could I? What do you mean—follow-through when you fart?"

"You know—brown skid marks," she made a wet farting sound.

Jeffrey looked shocked.

"Don't be so squeamish, Jeffrey—the joys of the geriatric—sounds like a movie—sponsored by Depends Adult Diapers!" She cackled with laughter.

"I wonder how Mr. Pilkington-Smith deals with difficult residents," she mused.

"He reminded me of Boner—Mr. Bohmer—Branscombe Hall master," Jeffrey said

"Can't say I remember him," said his mother.

"No, you wouldn't—weedy little character, totally unmemorable. But put a cane in his hand and he turned into an animal."

"What did he do?"

"He was quite the sight. Flecks of spittle at the corner of his mouth, a nervous twitch below one eye—eyes red with excitement. He could never resist one or two extra strokes. His shaking hands and clenched teeth showed just how difficult it was for him to stop."

"That's terrible! Did he ever cane you?"

"Oh yes. I was one of his favorites because I used to whimper and beg him to stop."

"Why didn't you tell me?"

"I was a wimp anyway. Squealing to the 'rents would have made me a double wimp. Boner wouldn't have stopped and I'd have gotten it from the other boys too."

Jeffrey's mother looked horrified.

"Look—here we are. This place is quite different from Shady Acres, I promise you."

Mrs. Keene looked out as they drove up in front of a large building masquerading as a cottage. A white picket fence enclosed chemical green grass on which garden gnomes and strolling plastic geese marched in line. Green and red shutters with heart-shaped cut-outs and flower boxes brimming with plastic pansies adorned every window. A large sign hanging on a curlicued wrought iron stand announced that they had arrived at *Ye Olde Rocking Chair.*

Jeffrey watched his mother, "Isn't this quaint?"

Mrs. Keene spluttered. She tried to say something but a paroxysm of laughter prevented her, so she just pointed a finger into her open mouth and made a gagging sound.

"Come on, Mother," Jeffrey said. "Give it a chance." He got out of the car and strode round to his mother's side and opened the door.

"No," Isabel said firmly. "I'm not getting out."

"Mother, you promised."

"I can't stand it when you whine, Jeffrey. Never could. Never will. Alright, I'll be a good girl. Can't be worse than Shady Acres."

The cloying smell of potpourri hit them as they opened the door. Jeffrey immediately began to sneeze. He pulled a handkerchief out of his pocket, noisily blew his nose and wiped his streaming eyes while his mother shook with laughter.

"They must have shares in Cozy Cottage Potpourri and Laura Ashley," she muttered.

The decor was busy. Pink and green vertical-striped wallpaper covered the walls to the half-way mark where a leafy border circled the room; above that, the walls were covered with a tiny floral print. The windows had balloon valances in the same fabric and white lacy sheers. The room was filled with an assortment of chairs, wingbacks, overstuffed loveseats and upright regency chairs, each one upholstered in a different fabric. Framed prints of red-cheeked children playing in apple orchards and embroidered sayings, like "Home is Where the Heart is," completed the picture.

"Well, this is very cozy, isn't it?" said Jeffrey.

Before his mother could respond, a large woman dressed in a voluminous Laura Ashley smock and contrasting print blouse, bustled into the room on a cloud of floral perfume. She stopped, fixed her eyes on Isabel, and dramatically held both her hands up to her cheeks.

"Oh my goodness! You're even more perfect than your lovely son's description. Yes, you'll love it here in our little family."

Both Jeffrey and his mother were speechless. Undaunted, the woman rushed on, reaching out to grasp both Isabel's hands. She was much bigger than Jeffrey's mother and she was one of those people who insisted on close-up conversation. Isabel's nose was inches away from the woman's formidable, floral chest.

"Oh, how rude of me," the woman pulled back a few inches without releasing Isabel's hands. "I haven't introduced myself. I'm Rosemary Fitzgerald—but everyone here calls me Mother Fitz." She snorted with laughter. "You've come at the perfect time—everyone's in the Crafts Room. Come and see."

She transferred her hold to Isabel's arm and propelled her along the corridor leading out of the lobby. "We have such fun here—you'll see." Jeffrey smiled reassuringly as his mother threw him a "help me" look over her shoulder.

Mother Fitz threw a door open and ushered Mrs. Keene inside. "Ta da!" she announced.

Isabel stared at the bulletin boards around the walls displaying drawings and crafts. People were grouped around tables, each one featuring a different activity—basket-weaving, clay modeling, collages. "Bloody eldergarten!" she snorted.

Noticeable by its absence was chatter, noise of any kind. The people slumped around the tables did not look up as they came in. A slight young man with thin blond hair threaded his way through the tables. Mother Fitz took his hand and pulled him toward Jeffrey's mother.

"Lionel, this is Isabel Keene—and Bell—it's alright if I call you Bell?—this is Lionel, our lion-hearted occupational therapist."

Lionel took Mrs. Keene's hand and gave it a weak squeeze.

"So what are we doing today, Lionel?"

Lionel gave Jeffrey a sidelong glance before going to a nearby table to pick up a lopsided basket in progress. "We're finishing off a variety of projects today. We're in-between themes right now," he added.

"We're **really** into themes here," Mother Fitz gushed. "I think Valentine's is my favorite. Everyone decorates their rooms, dresses in red or pink—we have red jello, pink punch, red chili beans."

"Pink bowel movements?" Jeffrey's mother asked innocently.

Mother Fitz and Lionel were momentarily taken aback, Jeffrey shot his mother a warning glance, but a rumpled old man in a wheelchair wheezed with laughter which turned into a paroxysm of coughing. Lionel looked at him anxiously as his face turned from red to purple before bustling over to a bank of pigeon holes on the wall, each one labeled with a first name. He reached into one marked Ricky and pulled out a pill bottle.

Mother Fitz's manner was distinctly cooler as they carried on with the tour. Isabel was now firmly in control, and the one-liners rolled off her tongue like laxative off a spoon.

"So you're telling me you have to have regency striped walls and floral drapes in your room even if the only color that lowers your blood pressure is turd brown?"

"I don't do low fat—hardly worth it at my age."

"Yes, I have quit. I stopped smoking in bed last year."

"That was very naughty, Mother," said Jeffrey as they drove away. Mrs. Keene waved regally at a confused Mother Fitz standing in the doorway of *Ye Olde Rocking Chair*. "Themed gerontology?" she muttered still smiling generously at Mother Fitz. "What next?"

Jeffrey just sighed and drove on.

Isabel was enjoying herself. She perched on the edge of her seat looking out. Jeffrey knew better than to remind her to fasten her seat belt.

"So where next? A sixties style hippy home? The Montessori Post-life Learning Centre? You know all this is a **huge** waste of time. I just want to stay in my own home 'til I fall off the perch."

Jeffrey sighed. "I know you do, Mother. But—"

"But I'm manic depressive," interrupted his mother. "That's all under control now."

"As long as you take the medication, and you know that you don't always do that, Ma."

"And? So what if I burn the house down while cooking hash brownies for Fred's 90th birthday bash?"

"Mother!"

"Well, it's better than suffocating inside a pumpkin outfit, or clogging the system with a surfeit of pink porridge."

"I saved the best for last, Ma," Jeffrey said with resignation. "You'll like this one."

"Oh, goody!"

They turned into a narrow driveway and drove up to a pleasant, mid-sized stone house.

"What? No name? No fancy sign?"

"No, it's just 49 Ridge Road."

"Well, that's a start."

An old man with an egg-stained cardigan and a walker was watering plants on the window-sill as they came into the entrance hall. He looked up and smiled. "Hello. You here to inspect the dump? Fred—Fred McIntyre," he nodded at his walker. "Can't shake your hand—fall on my arse if let go of this thing."

Jeffrey and his mother smiled. "Jeffrey Keene and this is my mother, Isabel."

"I'll give the old bag a call—MAGGIE! MAGGIE!" he shouted. "Some potential victims!"

He smiled at Jeffrey's mother, "Don't pay any attention to me. This place isn't too bad—I should know—third home for me—expelled for bad behavior!"

A door opened and a youngish woman in jeans and sweatshirt came in dusting flour off her hands.

"You trying your hand at cooking again, Maggie?—oh, oh—better go get the antacid."

"Have you been scaring these good people, Fred? The parsnips need thinning. Go and do something useful for a change," Maggie laughed.

"Slave driver," retorted Fred as he shuffled out. "I thought we were supposed to lie around and be waited on hand and foot until we die."

Maggie ushered them into a small room off the lobby. A desk in one corner was piled with papers and a half-eaten donut. The floor was covered with more papers, a tennis racket and shoes, a yellow Tonka truck and wooden blocks. Maggie lifted a fat marmalade cat off a small sofa and gestured for Jeffrey and his mother to sit down.

"Fred's a character, isn't he? But I'm glad you met him; kind of makes my job easier."

"He was very friendly," offered Jeffrey.

"Quite dishy," muttered his mother.

"He's a wonderful gardener—grows all our vegetables. Everyone helps out here if they can."

"What happens if they go gaga?" asked Isabel. "They get the chop?"

"Oh, Lord no. Residents can choose to do absolutely nothing, or they can take on a big job like the gardening, or they can just help when they feel like it."

"Doesn't that sound like a wonderful idea, Mother?" asked Jeffrey.

Isabel slapped him with her Ice Queen look.

"Someone's always around to chip in. Take today for example," Maggie gestured to her flour-covered apron. "Leslie usually bakes our pies—she makes the **best** pies. But she's having one of her anxiety attacks today and Hazel who often helps in the kitchen is—well her hemorrhoids are playing up—so I made the pies. Stay for dinner and you'll hear the groans."

"My feeling is," Maggie went on, "that our residents have paid their dues. If they want to stay in their rooms and sleep or rail at God then that's fine."

"Does Fred rail at God?" asked Isabel.

"Oh yes," laughed Maggie, looking sideways at a photo hanging on the wall.

Isabel followed her look. "Well, come on girl—what's the story?"

"Don't want to shock your son, do we?"

"Oh phooeey! He needs a bit of a shake down."

"Well," Maggie began. "Fred likes a drink every now and then—and that's fine here, incidentally. He's okay most of the time."

"And—? I know there's a story here," Isabel pressed.

"He did get a bit carried away during the spring planting. He was out-voted and had to put flowers and not potatoes in the front flower bed."

"And—what did he do?" asked Isabel impatiently.

Maggie looked at the photo again, hesitated, looked at Jeffrey, then took the photo down and handed it to Isabel.

At first glance, it was a normal photo of the front of the house with a large flower bed filled with purple and white petunias. But on closer look she could see that the flowers were arranged to spell something. She pulled the photo closer to make out the words. The blossoms spelled "F U 2 God!" She threw back her head in laughter and passed the photo to Jeffrey who looked at it and wordlessly passed it back to Maggie.

"And the best part was that I was the only person who noticed!" Maggie said as she put the photo back up on the wall.

"I have days like that sometimes," said Jeffrey's mother quietly.

"Yes, I know. Your son told me about your manic depression."

"But Mother's wonderfully creative," Jeffrey interrupted. "When we were young she would organize all the neighborhood pageants, musicals, skits—I thought you could do the same here, Ma."

Isabel began to look panicked. "That would be great." Maggie answered. "We've talked about doing that kind of thing—there's a lot of talent here. But we've never had anyone to organize us."

Isabel stood up, her face stony. "I would like to go home now, Jeffrey."

"But Mother," protested Jeffrey.

Maggie put her hand on Jeffrey's arm and shot him a warning glance. "I know you're not ready to give up your home and move in here, Isabel," she said, "but maybe you could come in occasionally and help us get some production off the ground. Fred has a vicious sense of humor and a great baritone voice."

"I'll see," Isabel said. "I have to go." She quickly left the room leaving a bewildered Jeffrey behind.

"Don't push her, Mr. Keene," Maggie said.

"But," Jeffrey began, and then he remembered sitting in the car with his parents outside Branscombe Hall.

"Do I have to, Ma?"

"Of course, you have to Jeffrey," answered his father. You don't want to grow up a dummy, do you? And that's what'll happen if you stay at the village school."

"You'll like it once you're here a while," cajoled his mother. "Lots of boys your own age—you can play in the band."

"And there's all the sports," added his father.

"But I can't even catch a ball."

"Maybe you'll learn how," his father said through clenched teeth.

He **had** learned to catch a ball, but never well enough to play on any of the school teams. And, despite Boner, despite some of the boys, it hadn't been all bad. He **had** kind of outgrown the village school, and maybe would have asked for a change a year or so later.

Jeffrey thanked Maggie and went out to the car where his mother was already sitting in the front seat, arms folded, ready for battle.

He looked over at her and smiled. "Don't worry, Ma— I'm not going to bully you. But you gotta admit, that last one wasn't half bad..."

"I **have to** admit, that last one was all right—you've got to watch out for these creeping Americanisms—ruined English, they have—ruined it."

"Let's go home, Ma. We'll buy some tea cakes on the way and you can toast them for me."

"Hope you like them burnt!"

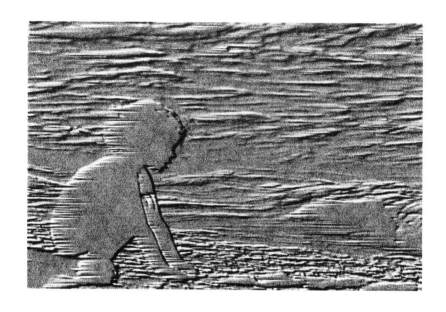

Strong and free, strong and free,
The floodgates are open, away to the sea.
Free and strong, free and strong,
Cleansing my streams as I hurry along,
To the golden sands, and the leaping bar,
And the taintless tide that awaits me afar,
As I lose myself in the infinite main,
Like a soul that has sinned and is pardoned again.
Undefiled, for the undefiled,
Play by me, bathe in me, mother and child.
—*Charles Kingsley*

Iona

*Ed. The following is an excerpt from Hazel Sangster's upcoming novel, **Iona**. Set on the Island of Iona in Scotland, the novel follows the journey of a middle-aged Canadian woman, Mairi Simpson, who has returned to the land of her ancestors in search of meaning in her life. She rents a house from Robert Stuart and is drawn into the tragedy surrounding him, his fey wife, Meg, and their mute son, Dougal. This chapter takes place at a ceilidh, an island party for everyone.*

Robert and Archie McPhail were sitting at the end of the pier, a very drunk Ian Cameron wedged between them. A strong norwesterly, laden with salt slapped their faces and tore the words out of their mouths. Archie had a flask in one hand and a thermos in the other. He passed the flask to Robert and poured a steaming cup of coffee which he pressed to Ian's lips.

"This'll keep you awake 'til next week, m'boy."

He held out his hand for the flask from Robert, took a hefty swig and replaced the silver, thistlehead stopper.

"Which'll come first —Ian sobering up or you and I falling dead drunk off the pier?" asked Robert laughing.

"Oh, you know Ian—he always rallies. Listen! He's starting to hum. That's always a good sign."

"Well, you know best Archie. How long have the two of you been playing together?"

"Who knows, Robert. As long as I can remember, our Da's played together. Mine was the drunk back then, God rest his soul. Ian's never played a note after my Da fell off Rhuach Ridge."

"You're a man of many talents, Archie. Looking at you slapping kids' hands for dipping into the gobstoppers in the shop, or ferrying flocks of queasy summer tourists out to your seals, who would guess you had music in your soul."

" I started playing for the seals, you know..."

"Come on, Archie, keep yon nonsense for the summerfolk and the Brigadier."

"I dinna deny that the tourists, especially the wimen folk, canna resist the dark pools of a silkie's eyes. Or that the Brig would wipe out the entire seal population to get one up on me. But it's not all a yarn. I'm no a religious man, or even a superstitious one. But I wouldnae harm a seal. She might be my dear departed Mam."

"Gimme that flask, Archie. I think you've had enough. Anyway we should be getting you down to the Hall—ceilidh's about to start."

Robert had inherited the job of organizing the ceilidhs. He wasn't an islander in the real sense. He hadn't been born on the Island. His family had lived on Mull for generations and had only left when they could no longer scratch out even a miserable subsistance. Since meeting Mairi, Robert often wondered what their life would have been like if they'd moved to Canada or Australia. His family only got as far as Glasgow. Glasgow hadn't been kind to them. Robert hated Glasgow. Even now, with its new sandblasted face, his heart sank every time he approached the Council flats on the outskirts of town. He could smell the boiling cabbage and drying diapers, hear his mother's complaining.

There was no future for him in Glasgow. The shipyards were closing, the pits were closing. Half the boys his age were out of work. Robert never knew what led him to Iona the summer he was fifteen. He just took the little money he had saved from working at the hardware store, hitched a ride to Oban and boarded the ferry. His Mam had died that summer. There was a picture on the wall at the undertakers. Robert had stared at that picture. It was just a photograph from a calendar—a typical West Highland sunset. It hadn't really made any great impression at the time—

or so Robert thought. But a couple of weeks later, with the house empty except for his red-eyed older sister and his glowering drunk of a father (the wee'uns had been shipped out to the foster home) it was to the balm of that scene that he ran.

He really lucked out on the Island. He met a man on the boat who saved his life. Callum Patterson—local crofter/poet/ fire chief/boat captain/ and ceilidh organizer. Callum hadn't asked any questions. He took Robert into his house, set him to work with the sheep and on the boats. Later he got him a real job, a paying job at the hotel. God, how he missed Callum! He hated the memory of him at the end, eaten away by the cancer, remembering him as the colossus he first saw standing against the late afternoon sun on the bow of the King George V ferry.

Up at the Iona Community Hall people were beginning to arrive. Shapes huddling under large black umbrellas crowded into the little entrance way, stamping feet, wiping water off faces, shedding rubber boots and oilskins.

"Fair peltin' down."

"Ay"

"Jamie."

"Jock." The men greeted each other with a nod.

The women shed their coats, twitched bows in daughters' hair and wiped drips off little noses. Then they picked up their newspaper-wrapped plates and trays of food and went to the kitchen at the back of the hall.

"So who's met this Canadian woman, then?"

"Is she coming tonight?"

"Where's Edna? She'll know."'

"Oh my! Here she is! Just look at yon dress."

"And new, white high heels..."

"**And** matching purse."

"What's on the trays, Edna?"

"Smells good."

"What about this Mairi Simpson then, Edna?"

"Just a minute, girls. Let me get my bridies into the oven."

"Two whole trays of bridies!"

"Willie! Get your thieving mitts out of there. Go play with your sisters."

"Well? Come on, Edna. Have you met her?"

Edna perched herself on the edge of the kitchen table in her shiny pink dress with matching bow, her legs swinging gaily. The others crowded round.

"Yes I have. She came to the shop the other day, and we had a nice wee chat."

"Well? What does she look like?"

"How old is she?"

"Is she married?"

"One question at a time, ladies. Oh thanks, Heather. A dram is welcome on a night like this."

Edna took a dainty sip of her drink in its plastic cup.

"I'd say she's around 45. She's a big build, but I wouldnae say she was fat. Maybe she was fat—once. Her skin looks too big. She's got a pretty face. Her hair was a mess, mind you, and she looks the sort that nivver wears make up. She's no a cheery person."

"Probably running away from something, then."

"You still havenae told us if she's married or not?"

"Dinna fash yourself, Agnes. She's no the type Rory usually goes after!"

"Come on, Edna, tell us."

"Yes, she's married and she's even a Gran. Her oldest daughter is married with a wee'un and her son plays in a rock band."

"But what's she doing here, wi'out her husband?"

"And in November?"

"She just said she wanted a holiday and that her husband was too busy to get away." Edna was enjoying the audience. "She used to come here as a bairn. She was born in Scotland, you know."

"If I had the money for a wee holiday I would go to the Costa Brava—somewhere hot."

"My cousin Aggie went there last year and she said it was turrible."

"The food's all greasy and there's flies everywhere."

"And even the policemen pinch your bum."

Jeannie McPhail interrupted. "I heard from Fiona up at the hotel that the Canadian woman came because she dreamed about Iona..."

All interest now turned to Jeannie.

"She did?"

"A dream? Well that explains it..."

"What kind of a dream?"

Before answering, Jeannie took a bite of one of the shortbread squares she was laying out. "You know Fiona, she's nae one to pry, but she said that Meg and Dougal were in the dream—helping the Canadian woman find something she'd lost."

"She's no a happy woman, that's all I ken," said Edna.

The women fell silent, nodding gently, each thinking of some sadness deep in their own hearts.

Robert and Archie McPhail managed to walk Ian Cameron from the pier and install him on the stage at the back of the hall underneath the pictures of the Queen and Bonnie Prince Charlie.

That picture of the Queen was the only thing that ever came close to tearing the Island apart. It wasn't that the islanders didn't like the Queen as a person; she was doing a fine job, under the circumstances. It dated back to 1953 when they first hung the picture with its inscription "Elizabeth II". Elizabeth I of England was not popular on the island. Back then, Mary was the rightful Queen of Scotland. The islanders would never forgive Elizabeth for chopping off Mary's head in 1587. (Robert remembered his Aunt Elsie's indignation when Elizabeth was crowned Queen in

1953. She was so incensed by the **II** on the mailboxes that she had gone around stuffing burning newspaper into them). The ensuing argument made it all the way to the London papers and only died down when someone (rumor said it was Callum Patterson) removed the inscription. Edna Bain bought a picture of Mary Queen of Scots in Oban and put it at the other end of the hall, so the two of them got to look at each other across the centuries.

Archie McPhail was spilling over the edges of the small metal chair on the stage. His legs in their hairy green kilt socks were like two moss covered stumps. He hugged his accordion to his belly and moved his huge hands surprisingly quickly over the keys. He was sweating already. Ian Cameron was wedged upright on his chair with cushions. He sat very straight, fiddle under his chin, eyes closed. He never stopped playing, just went straight from one tune to another. Archie joined in after a bar or so. On the chair between them were two tumblers of whiskey, and two cups of coffee.

"Grand job, Robert."

Robert turned to see Ian Davidson in his kilt and clerical collar. He gestured to the glass of pale whiskey in his hand. "Getting those two to play is like making a good malt. It needs a Master Blender!"

Robert laughed. "I reckon there's a pretty good blend between the malt and blood in Ian's veins right now!"

"The man's a great fiddler."

"Did you hear what happened at the Mod last year? The first day he was so sober he forgot the tune. The next day his playing was inspired, but he fell off the stage when he was accepting the Silver Fiddle from Lady Crichton-Stewart!"

"The Lord moves in mysterious ways!"

Despite the umbrella, Mairi and Dougal were thoroughly wet and cold by the time they walked down the track to the village hall. Their steps quickened, drawn by the lights beaming out of every window. The sound of the fiddle and the accordion battled with the wind gusts and the smell of firewood and roasting lamb.

Dougal took off as soon as they were in the door. Mairi watched as he headed straight for a tray of steaming pies and grabbed two before the woman standing beside them—it was the woman from the post office—could scold him.

Mairi took off her jacket and hung up the umbrella. She hugged the wall and inched into the crowded room. The familiar feelings of panic at being in a room full of people who weren't talking to her welled up. But before she had time to really regret coming, Robert was at her elbow guiding her into the packed room. Chairs lined the walls. Robert gestured to two old men sitting side by side.

"That's Angus Stewart, our local laird. He owns the island—hasn't put the rents up for thirty years."

Mairi took in the poker straight back, shaggy white eyebrows over bright eyes. Itchy tweed suit, flannel shirt that didn't meet at the neck. Faded tartan tie with porridge stains on it. The kind of face that people trust.

"The one next to him is Dougie Abercrombie. If you walk to Fingal's Point you can see him there sitting in the Lady Caroline. That's his boat. She's beached now. He's there every day, rain or shine, in his patched yellow oilskin and the cap with the torn gold braid, puffing his pipe and looking across the firth to Rum and Eigg."

The two men weren't actually talking. They were nodding to each other, like two babies she had seen in their carriages outside Woolworth's. The music started up and the nodding heads and tapping toes took up the beat of the reel.

Mairi felt tug at her skirt. It was Dougal and he wanted to dance.

"It's Strip the Willow—Dougal's favorite," Robert explained.

"But I don't know how to dance Scottish reels."

"Dougal'll keep you straight. Go on, it's fun," Robert coaxed.

Dougal pulled Mairi into the dance. It looked horribly complicated, but Mairi found that, if she relaxed, she was passed from one arm to another like a rag doll, spun on one beat and let go opposite her next partner.

She danced a lot that evening, with almost everyone on the Island it seemed. She did the Statue Waltz with little Malcolm McAllister who asked her how many times she'd been attacked by Indians with bows and arrows. She did the Dashing White Sergeant with Dougal and Mrs. Davidson, who was resplendent in a voluminous, floor length kilt.

"It's a dance for three people," Mrs. Davidson explained.

Mairi finished an energetic polka, pressed against a burly purple sweater whose name she never caught. She needed a rest. It was stuffy in the little hall, so she went outside and sat down for a few minutes on a bench. The rain had stopped although it was still windy.

Haven't danced like that for years. Out of breath. Out of shape. Have I ever danced like that? Wild waltzes with Mom in the kitchen on snowy afternoons. Short legs spinning against Mom's long legs. Ages ago.

I don't like dancing Mairi, Nigel said.

You could have fooled me—and all the others who were watching you and that blond in the backless dress do that foxtrot, I said.

Bosses have to dance with their secretaries, Mairi. Surely you know that by now.

It looked as though you'd been dancing together for years. Everyone stopped to look at you.

"Getting a breath of fresh air, then?"

Mairi jumped. She hadn't heard Robert come up beside

her. "Oh! You startled me! Where did you come from?"

"I took Angus home. He had a big heart operation last year and he's supposed to take it easy. Hard for a man like him. He lost his wife last year—now he's got the whole Island looking out for him!"

"You're all so kind to each other here," mused Mairi, almost to herself.

"And you seem to be a hit with everyone," said Robert. "I don't think you've been off the dance floor once."

Back inside, Robert shifted his sporran to one side and they began to dance. He shouldn't have been such a natural dancer with his big hands and big feet. His strong hand in the small of Mairi's back, the rough cloth of his kilt sweeping against her skirt, she let the plaintive music reach far inside her. The song ended on a long quavering note from the fiddle.

"I have to get back to the bar. I left Dougal in charge. He either pours triples or forgets to put any of the hard stuff in at all! Have you eaten yet? Phoebe Tindall's Scotch eggs are legendary."

Mairi began to laugh. "Food! I haven't even thought about eating! Not once!"

Robert wasn't even sure why she was laughing, but he joined in just the same. "Well, come and have something now."

"Thanks, Robert. I'm not hungry. I've really enjoyed this evening. Much more than I expected. I'm usually not big on parties. But I'm kind of tired. I think I'll just walk home."

"Will you manage on your own? I could get Dougal to..."

"Thanks. I'll be fine."

"Could I perhaps? I was wondering if I could ask you a favo r? I could ask Dougal, but he's having such a good time, the mite—could you look in on Meg for me?"

"Of course. Should I stay with her?"

"Oh, no. There's no need for that. She should be sleeping. Sometimes she's a mite restless at night. She'll take some hot milk and bread and butter if she's awake."

Mairi was oddly flattered to be asked to look in on Meg—surprised too. She rarely asked people for favors. But it seemed natural here on Iona.

"The door to the house is off the latch", continued Robert. "Just go right on in. And thank you."

The track up the hill was wet and muddy and Mairi had to pick her way around the puddles. Every few minutes a full moon came out from behind the dark clouds that were blowing wildly around the sky. The wind had whipped the sea into huge waves. Mairi could hear them crash on the shore. Tomorrow she would take a walk over to the other side of the Island.

Sure enough, the Stuart farmhouse door was not locked and a light was burning in the hallway. She went through the main room to the back of the house. She opened the door to one room barely bigger than a cupboard, inside an old iron bed heaped with clothes and blankets. The floor was covered with little boxes full of rocks, shells, feathers, twigs—must be Dougal's room. The next room was slightly bigger. There were no curtains on the windows. Mairi could see Meg MacLean as she lay asleep.

So young. Just like Dougal. Skin like wax. Touch her to make sure she's warm. She looks so normal. Does she dream? Of her lost baby? She's looks so peaceful. She's even smiling. Wish I could be this still, this quiet inside. Is it warm in your world, Meg? Is it safe? Can't imagine losing my child. Not now. Not then, when he was a baby. Is there a deep place of pain forever inside you? I feel that pain, that emptiness. Can't walk away from it. Share it. Lie down beside you. Soft hair. Warm breath. Safe smell.

Meg stirred and turned on one side, reaching out in her sleep to put an arm around Mairi and pull her close.

They were both asleep like that when Dougal and Robert

came home from the ceilidh. Robert moved as if to wake her, but Dougal stayed his hand with his own and shook his head. He crawled onto the bottom of the bed and curled himself up. Robert brought a blanket from Dougal's room and covered him. "Goodnight, son." He kissed him, then Meg, and stood looking down at the bed. He bent down and brushed a lock of Mairi's hair back from her face and gently touched her cheek with the back of his hand. "Too bad there's no room for me." He smiled. He caught Dougal's look. "I know. Don't be daft, Dad,'" he mimicked. He sighed and went out, closing the door quietly.

For Marcia: 1938-1992

When I think of you
I think of
Water
Waves
Rolling
One after the other
Never missing a beat
Smoothing every time
The troubled sands
Erasing the sad footprints of life.

When I think of you
I think of
Sunlight
Pushing through the brooding storm clouds
Tipping the waves of the lake you love so well with
Light
Hope
Joy.

When I think of you
I think of
Earth
Freshly ploughed fields
Birds circling to feast
Rich dark dirt clinging to boots
And the roots of
Vegetables
Sweet with life.

When I think of you
I think of
Fire
Blazing through the window on a wintry day
Crackling up to the summer stars
Family, friends, strangers
Hands outstretched to your
Warmth
Energy
Love.

Other Books available from Savage Press

Hometown Wisconsin by Marshall Cook

Treasures from the Beginning of the World by Jeff Lewis

Stop in the Name of the Law by Alex O'Kash

Widow of the Waves by Bev Jamison

Stop and Smell the Cedars by Tony Jelich

Voices from the North Edge by St. Croix Writers

Gleanings from the Hillsides by E.M. Johnson

Keeper of the Town by Don Cameron

Mystic Bread by Mike Savage

The Lost Locomotive of the Battle-Axe by Mike Savage

Moments Beautiful Moments Bright by Brett Bartholomaus

Total Eclipse by Judith James

Some Things You Never Forget by Clem Miller

The Courtship of Sarah McLean by S. & S. Castleberry

To order additional copies of
Thicker Than Water
or receive the complete
Savage Press catalog

Talk to us at:

Tel: 1-800-READ TNR
(1-800-732-3867)
Fax: (715) 394-9513
email: savpress@delphi.com
See our Web Page at:
www.cp.duluth.mn.us/~awest/savpress

Visa or MasterCard accepted

PRESS

Box 115, Superior, WI 54880 (715) 394-9513

We are always looking for good manuscripts—poetry,
fiction, memoir, family history, true crime and other genres.
Send a synopsis and the first three chapters.